that she could spend the remainder of existence with the man unlucky enough to love her.

"After you died, Elise carried your body throughout Hell," James had explained. "For weeks, she bore your weight in search of a cure that could never be found, dragging you through battles and mourning in her way."

And when she had become God—because that was what the Godslayer had become by the time James told Seth the truth—she had decided to bring Seth back to life.

That would have been fine, in theory, if Elise hadn't decided to bring Seth back like *her*.

A god.

There were always three gods. A human. An angel. A demon.

Elise had been human again, and James had always had the blood of an angel.

That had only left one role Seth could play.

Resurrecting him had satisfied Elise's guilt, and it had damned him for eternity.

He'd have rather stayed dead.

Niflheimr, The Winter Court—December 2030

There was a day that Marion spilled so much blood that she couldn't stand.

The wards of Niflheimr required blood. Soul links, they were called. A strange kind of magic with origins predating Genesis, bearing all the dark potential of that era.

By bleeding into the wards, Marion gave herself to the magic, and the magic gave back exponentially.

Establishing a strong connection was difficult for a mage with no sidhe blood. The altars acknowledged her authority—she was steward, after all—but all the raw power in the world could only go so far because it was the wrong power.

So Marion spilled blood. A lot of it. And she'd only had so much to give, because she had already bled for other purposes in recent weeks: bleeding because Arawn's Hounds had tried to kill her, bleeding because Seth had drunk from her sleeping throat.

She gave all she had, though.

Niflheimr stood strong in thanks.

She needed days to recover, and she spent those days in bed, drinking endless amounts of water and taking lengthy naps. During that time, Konig handled political issues. The business of becoming a royal family couldn't be put on pause, even for such necessary evils as blood magic.

There was one day that Konig took off, though. Meetings were canceled or delegated to Nori. He crawled into bed with a bowl of soup he'd made himself—which tasted wretched, though Marion was so touched that she drank it anyway.

They spent that entire day in bed together, fully clothed, beneath a suspended cage of ice sculptures. They were warmed within the canopy of veils by their breaths and combined body heat, creating beads of condensation like diamonds shivering on the tips of icicles.

Konig whispered their history on her fingertips while her arm was coiled around his jaw to stroke his cheek.

"We met because you came to the party to celebrate the Alpha's reelection," he murmured, "and you wore a white dress."

She almost remembered it when she stared hard enough at the icicles. Even if memory failed her, she could use his words to construct the memories out of ether. What a shock it must have been to see a face as perfect as Konig's among the crowd of politicians and celebrities and members of the mainstream media.

"There were people between us. Knots of them. I knew they were gathered around somebody I couldn't see, and my friend told me it was you. The bodies parted, and you were there. You wore a white dress." His breath fogged between them. Marion scried through the abstract shapes—the crowd, the white dress, and then Konig, angular and slouching and graceful. A rock star. A prince.

Her prince.

"We kissed the first time that same night." His fingers played through the folds of her skirt, letting it fall from his hand like autumn leaves from the branches.

Konig continued to speak throughout the day, illustrating the moments that formed the foundation of their relationship.

He described the breakfast they'd shared after their first night together. Konig and Marion had gazed at one another in wonder from chairs that had felt positioned too far apart, wondering if there were any way that the others in the court wouldn't be able to feel the chemistry between them.

Their second night had been better for both of them. Their bodies had remained mysterious and new, but Konig had already known that Marion liked it when he touched her throat. When he explained that, he stroked the lacework of veins under her skin. Her pulse responded by beating against his thumb.

He progressed to when Marion had next seen his parents at court. She'd known them longer than she'd known Konig, working with Violet and Rage as a peer despite their disparate ages. She'd returned as the lover of their son and they'd known, instinctively. The sidhe knew nothing better than sex.

"So awkward," Konig said, and they giggled at each other, curled up in the sheets together.

It was a wonder, this recreation of their love. They'd gotten so few idle moments together that stealing an entire idle day felt like sin. Old history made new.

They kissed while they talked, tangled in each other. Lips on forehead. Lips on chin. Lips on fingertips.

Marion could see why she had fallen in love with him. She fell in love with him again.

The idle day ended. Marion recovered and politics returned.

There was no resurrecting the romance they'd lost, but Marion felt the ghost of it living on in Konig's heart. As long as he remembered, that was all Marion needed. Knowing their love survived in him made meetings with enemy states so much warmer.

Marion and Konig loved one another, true love, in the way of epic poems—love that could have shattered worlds. More powerfully still, they loved each other in the way of a teenage boy and a teenage girl for whom reality was more tenuous than the future they imagined together.

Soon to be King and Queen of the Winter Court.

Married until death parted them.

TWO

Billings, Montana—January 2031

The last time that Marion Garin had been in a hospital, she'd had several intrusive tests performed. She'd been asked to spill quantities of blood minute in comparison to what soul links required. She'd also had to lie within a rumbling MRI machine for long, aching minutes. And she'd been forced to sit in a room alone, waiting for results from those tests.

It turned out that the intrusion had been to no avail. Marion had only learned she was a half-angel.

She'd also learned that she desperately, urgently needed a man named Dr. Lucas Flynn in her life. At the time, she hadn't known *why* she needed him. She hadn't known much of anything, in fact. What few memories she possessed had been formed in the weeks following the hospital.

Marion still had far more questions than answers.

She entered Hitchens Valley General Hospital to get a few more answers, though they wouldn't be produced by having her blood drawn or her body scanned.

These answers, she hoped, would come from a man named Geoff Samuelson. He was a werewolf who had been considered a John Doe until his photo pinged government facial recognition software. Two months earlier, he'd been found comatose outside of a club called Original Sin. He hadn't woken up since then.

She slipped into his hospital room to find the lights dimmed and his immobile form swaddled in blankets. The bed sighed as it inflated and deflated in turn. That function was intended to prevent bedsores in patients who would likely remain hospitalized indefinitely.

"Hello, Geoff." Marion sank onto the edge of his bed, the voluminous layers of her red dress billowing around her legs before coming to rest like a fog of blood.

"Do you need anything?" Nori Harper, Marion's cousin and her shadow as of late, was hanging back in the doorway.

"Privacy, please," Marion said.

Nori stepped back and shut the door.

Marion leaned her weight on one arm as she studied Geoff Samuelson's face. Unconscious, the werewolf was unassuming. The doctors had estimated that he was a man of roughly forty years, and the many healed fractures in his skeleton suggested previous military service. That may have been true, but Marion suspected some old wounds had been incurred in his work as a mercenary.

The doctors knew very little else about Geoff. The only reason Marion knew more was because her adopted sister, Dana McIntyre, got around in mercenary circles. Dana's dossier said that Geoff's lycanthropy predated Genesis. He was bitten—a cursed werewolf—unlike many shapeshifters, who had been changed by will of the gods or born preternatural.

Marion could see the silvery-white scarring from Geoff's original werewolf bite when she tilted her head. She wondered if the violence of the change might have tipped him over the emotional cliff that had led to his assassin work.

He'd been hired to kill Marion. The money must have been good, if not good enough to risk losing his life to a coma.

Marion hooked her forefinger in his nasal cannula and extracted it from his nostrils. Oxygen breezed over his upper lip. "Time to wake up, Geoff."

She rubbed her hands together while summoning magic. Marion had forgotten all her magical abilities along with her memories, but she'd flung herself into studying the matter as only a half-angel could while bed-bound with anemia. She'd read every book and internet article she could locate on the subject. Luckily, since Genesis had forced even generations-old covens into the public eye, the amount of information available was truly staggering.

Marion's studies had revealed that normal witches—people who were fully human—could gather magical energy from nature's bounty. They preferred focused energy from herbs and crystals, but anything in the world would do. For a half-angel mage like Marion, her options were endless.

There were plains outside of Hitchens Valley: seemingly endless miles of rolling grass inhabited primarily by cows. That was where Marion drew from.

She inhaled the life energy from the plains, the sun beating upon the winter-chilled snow, foxes darting through tunnels in the soil.

Her hands glowed.

"Geoff," Marion called, reaching into his mind. "Come to me, Geoff."

Magic of the mind couldn't be learned on the internet. It was something she drew from within herself, tapping into the wellspring of ethereal blood that flowed through her veins.

She extended her reach into the core of Geoff's unconscious mind.

Memories swirled under the matte wall of unconsciousness. They were wisps of smoke from an extinguished candle. At least he had those wisps. Marion had nothing but holes.

She reached past the memories and tapped his gray matter.

Life sparked through his mind.

The doctors had been unable to determine a medical cause for his coma, and that was because there was no medical cause. Geoff had been turned off like a computer with the plug yanked out the back. Marion couldn't tell if the cause was magical or something godlier. It didn't really matter. Once she found the place where consciousness had been disconnected, it was easy enough to reconnect.

Marion plugged him in.

Geoff's eyes opened. He sucked in a breath that made color flush his cheeks. He clawed reflexively at the starchy bed sheets, the monitors on his chest, the cannula now tickling his chin.

"Hush, you're okay." Marion kept stroking his forehead.

He honed in on her voice. His golden eyes focused on Marion's face, and recognition struck moments later. "Shit!"

"Hush," she said again, pressing her hand to his chest. "Give yourself a moment to relax."

He shook his head wildly and pressed his back against the mattress, fingers clutching the sheets. "You're—it's you—you're the target who—"

"Yes, I'm the woman you tried to kill. Consider yourself forgiven."

Confusion contorted his face. The lines were deeper than they should have been at his age. He'd lost weight from being fed intravenously, and it aged him relative to the OPA's photos. "I'm forgiven?"

"You didn't succeed," Marion pointed out.

He still didn't relax, nor could he escape. Even a werewolf with preternatural strength seemed to have suffered atrophy from his coma. "What do you want?"

"I want to talk." She took a cup from his bedside, filled it with water from the sink, and dabbed a sponge in it. She stuck it between his lips.

Geoff sucked mistrustfully. "I don't know who put the hit out," he said when she set the cup and sponge down again.

"That's not what I want to talk about." The hit was old news at that point. The leader of the angels, Leliel, had happily claimed responsibility for the bounty. Leliel had hoped to prevent Marion from sharing the will of the gods with the world. She'd failed as surely as Geoff had.

"I don't know anything about *anything*," Geoff said.

"You know more than I do. You know what happened that night outside of Original Sin because you were there."

"So were you."

"Indulge me, please. Tell me what you remember." She couldn't help but utter the last word with some longing.

Geoff lifted a hand as though to rub his face, then stopped. He couldn't move that far with the IV in his wrist. "I took a train to Billings. Me and Vasicek, we took the train together. Wait— Vasicek—is he—?"

"Dead."

Geoff didn't look disturbed. "We found you because you'd emailed another woman about meeting her."

Marion knew that part. She had gone to Original Sin to talk to Nori in neutral territory. Vasicek had fired into the crowd in order to drive Marion into the back alley, where Geoff had been waiting to kill her. Nori had been able to relate all the details up to that point.

After that, things became fuzzier.

Marion only knew that someone had killed Vasicek, disabled Geoff, and stolen her memories. She didn't know who or how. "Someone attacked me after you left, and I believe you saw it. You're the only one who may have seen it."

"I did, but she didn't attack you. All I saw was that you talked to her."

Her heart leapt. She had begun to suspect who might have taken her memories weeks earlier, when she'd returned from the Nether Worlds. Who would have had the strength to defeat Marion? Who could have excised her memories and jammed them into an artifact like the Canope?

Probably the same people who had sent Marion after Seth Wilder—the man who was most likely the third god of the triad.

Geoff's use of a female pronoun made Marion think specifically of her half-sister, the woman who had once been Godslayer. Elise Kavanagh.

"Tell me everything you saw," Marion said.

"I saw..." He stared blankly at the ceiling.

Words failed him. He shook his head. "I don't know what I saw." Thoughts flickered over the surface of his mind. He knew what he saw. He just didn't want to say it.

"Tell me," she urged.

He shook his head again.

Marion glanced at the clock at his bedside. She was too busy to coerce honesty from a petty mercenary. As a half-angel, she should have been capable of simply plucking the knowledge from his mind, but she had overextended herself waking him up. She was still weak from the sanguine needs of Niflheimr's wards.

Luckily, Marion had access to some enchantments she'd cast before losing her memory. She extracted a metal bracelet from her pocket and clasped it on Geoff's wrist. Magic sparked.

"Tell me what you saw," she said again.

Spells seethed within the atoms of the bracelet, shooting swirling tendrils into Geoff's mind. That magic was capable of compelling truth from anyone who wore it.

Even petty mercenaries.

"A goat," Geoff said.

"A goat? Not a woman who looks like me, but with redder hair?" Marion asked.

"She was the size of a child, with creepy little human hands, and a goat head. I know it sounds stupid. I feel stupid saying it. You'd just thrown me across an alley with lightning, so chances are pretty good I was imagining stuff, but that's what I saw. A goat-woman."

He couldn't be lying. The bracelet made that impossible.

But a "cloaked goat-woman" was impossible, too.

Nobody should have been able to defeat Marion except her godly half-sister.

She slipped the bracelet from his wrist again, and only then did Geoff seem to realize what he had done. He looked angry. "You happy?"

"I'm grateful." She pocketed the bracelet. "Thank you, Mr. Samuelson. You've been most helpful."

"Get me doctors," Geoff said. "I want out of here. I want my family."

"You'll be out of here soon enough."

Marion didn't shut the door behind her when she left.

There were agents from the Office of Preternatural Affairs waiting in the hallway with Nori. They were easily distinguished from hospital staff by their all-black clothing, lapel pins with the sword-and-shield logo, and their enchanted guns.

Marion had been forced to call in several favors to get access to Geoff Samuelson before his arrest. They'd given her five minutes—generous, considering they'd owed her none.

"You can have him now," Marion said to the nearest of the agents. "Thank you for your help."

The woman in charge, Agent Bryce, didn't meet Marion's eyes. Like most people, she seemed to find the ice-blue of angelic irises unsettling.

"Thank you, ma'am."

Marion stepped aside to let the agents move into Geoff's room.

Nori rose from a chair, wringing her hands together. "Did you learn what you needed?"

"Yes," Marion said. She wasn't wearing the bracelet, but that was the truth.

Marion had learned what she needed, even if the information wasn't exactly what she wanted.

Nori carried Marion to Niflheimr, arriving on the landing pad that they'd chosen as the safest point of entry into the world. It was the most intact balcony they'd been able to locate in the sprawling towers, and reasonably near to the throne room. They'd placed plywood across the holes in the floor for safety's sake, but Marion still shuddered when she reappeared with her toes inches from one edge. She took a hurried step back.

Niflheimr had been grown through magic, and that meant the balcony was at a height only reachable through magic, too. If Marion fell, she'd have a long time to regret it before smashing into the frozen ocean.

Nori whipped furs out of a chest just inside the tower and settled them over Marion's shoulders. "Five minutes. Do the wards quickly."

"I don't need to be reminded," Marion said without any anger. She didn't *need* to be reminded, but it didn't hurt these days. It was impossible to tell what Marion would know and what she didn't. Part of her had been killed in Sheol and could never be resurrected.

Nori's reminder helped on another level. It was tempting not to refresh the soul-linked wards even though they'd placed an altar on the balcony to make the ritual as convenient as possible— which was not convenient at all. There was nothing convenient about having to bleed every time she returned to the Winter Court. When Nori prompted Marion, she couldn't pretend to forget.

Marion took a dagger from the altar. She slashed her palm and blood dribbled down her wrist. Magic shocked through Marion when she touched the altar, opening her mind.

In that instant, the icy towers were her bones. The frozen ocean was her flesh. The forest, from the Coronal Ridge to the Wilds, was her hair, her eyelashes, her fingernails.

Her hand was healed when she stepped away, but not before she'd spilled a fair amount of blood. Again. Just as she had every time she left and returned to the Winter Court.

Every time, the shock of magic was weaker. The wards were weaker. They weren't intended to be linked to the soul of someone who wasn't sidhe, after all.

Nori was wringing her hands again. "Did it work?"

"It worked this time." No promises for next time. "Lead the way."

Nori led Marion down the tower's spiraling stairs to the courtyard. They'd temporarily housed refugees there, but the only remaining sign of their camp was a memorial commissioned from unseelie artists. Marion had been quick to have the wreckage from Leliel's assault tidied by the Raven Knights.

Another of the unseelie families had returned to the courtyard to mourn that day. Marion recognized Rhiannon and Morrighan, a pair of sidhe who had originally been found in Leiptr. They were sobbing over fresh additions to the memorial: a photo of an old man hugging a girl surrounded by candles, flowers, and sprigs of berries.

"Three minutes." Nori tapped her wrist even though she didn't wear a watch.

"I know." But Marion didn't follow Nori. She longed to join the grieving families and offer another apology. A thousand more apologies. There weren't enough apologies in the universe for the harm Marion had inflicted upon them with her selfishness.

Rhiannon and Morrighan weren't the only ones in the courtyard, though. A small figure flitted through the shadows beyond twisted columns.

It was a boy-child who was perhaps five feet tall and well built for a six year old. He was camouflaged against the icy castle by his blue skin, translucent hair, and dark eyes. Ymir was a young frost giant born after Genesis who had never known anything but the Winter Court, and one of the few witnesses who had survived Leliel's attack on Niflheimr.

He hadn't spoken to Marion since the deaths. Not once.

"Two and a half minutes," Nori said with more urgency.

Ymir was looking her way with obvious longing, and Marion owed him so much. The least she could give him was her time.

But then Ymir looked over Marion's shoulder. His eyes widened.

He turned and vanished into the halls.

"Princess," said a masculine voice.

Marion turned to find Prince ErlKonig of the Autumn Court striding down the stairs.

Even now, he took her breath away. The sidhe were hedonists in the truest sense of the word, reveling in all things self-indulgent and luxurious, and the bloodlines bred with similar priorities. Konig had been birthed from Genesis with all the beauty that the faerie courts could muster.

Perfectly symmetrical features were framed by blue-black hair that shouldn't have matched his coppery skin or the high-saturation violet of his irises. The colors should have looked ridiculous, even on a man attractive enough to grace the cover of any magazine on Earth.

Konig didn't look ridiculous, though. Especially not when he was looking at Marion like...*that*. With that heat in his eyes. Like the energy between them might melt all of Niflheimr.

It was a wonder that the Winter Court hadn't been baked into summer with the heat that flowed between them.

He was holding a bloodstained card in one hand.

"We have a problem," Konig said.

Marion stretched onto her toes to kiss him. He tasted of the spiced wine made in his childhood home of the Autumn Court. Konig normally had a sensuous way of moving his lips that brought intimate things to Marion's mind—and between her legs—but he was restrained today.

He must have been worried.

"What is it?" Marion asked.

He lifted the card so she could see. It was one of the invitations for their impending nuptials. "A message."

She took the card with the nails of her forefinger and thumb to avoid touching the blood. Someone had written "I'm coming for you" on the RSVP line. It was edged with jagged warlock runes, the dark mirror image of the angel magic Marion should have been able to cast.

"It's Arawn," Konig said. "He's planning to strike our wedding."

The jagged lightning strikes of the letters scorched into the stationary did look rather Arawn-like, but it wasn't signed. "We've gotten threats from too many sources to say that this one is coming from him."

"I know for a fact that this came from Arawn." Konig raised his voice to a shout. "Heather!"

His favorite personal guard, Heather Cobweb, descended the same stairs that he had. She wore pants of fox-fur and her hair in two long braids. She was also carrying the corpse of a massive white dog across her shoulders. Its furry ears were tipped in a shade of red similar to the blood on the invitation. "I found this dead on the edge of the Wilds."

"Gods above!" Marion stepped back even faster than when she'd been trying to avoid the holes in the balcony above. The white dog was a Hound—one of Arawn's. They'd nearly killed Marion in Sheol. "How did Arawn get that close?"

Heather let the dog slide from her shoulders. It flopped to the ground at her feet. "I have no clue. But there it was, among the trees with that note attached to its collar."

I'm coming for you.

Marion shivered and hugged her arms around herself. "Why would he want to attack our wedding?"

"My first guess? Revenge," Konig said. He and Arawn had clashed in the Nether Worlds. Konig had walked away winner and Arawn was too prideful to let such an insult stand.

"What's your second guess?"

"The darknet," Heather said. "He must think he'll be able to get people into Niflheimr to attend the wedding, and then he could go after the servers."

The darknet was a private network that connected preternaturals across all Middle

Worlds and Nether Worlds, and mercenaries found their marks on its forums. That was where Leliel had posted the bounty that had led Geoff Samuelson to attack Marion.

Everyone said that the darknet servers were housed in the Winter Court, but Marion hadn't seen them. True, Niflheimr was labyrinthine, so it was possible they were still hidden. Possible, but unlikely. "Arawn is much too smart to wage war over servers that nobody is certain are in the Winter Court, and we have no reason to take such a leap in logic for his motivation."

"Not too much a leap. We know for a fact that the servers have put a target on your royal backs." Heather stroked a hand through the fur of the dead Hound. "The guest you're about to meet brought an entourage with her, and the Raven Knights already caught one of them snooping in the dungeons. Jolene Chang claimed to be lost, but..."

The dungeons were so far from the social areas of Niflheimr that Marion couldn't find them without help of a map.

"You think she was looking for the servers too?" Marion asked.

"Guarantee it. The AGC has been trying to shut the darknet down for years. They're taking advantage of your diplomatic handshake to take another shot at it."

"That doesn't say anything about Arawn," Nori said. "What can we do about him?" Marion had forgotten that her half-angel assistant was still there. Nori had been lurking near the edge of the courtyard looking miserable ever since Marion and Konig's intimate greeting.

"For now, we must attend our meeting and ask about Jolene Chang," Konig said. "But after that..." He glared at the Hound.

After that, they'd have to contemplate what a dead Hound meant, and what Arawn might do to their wedding.

"Let's go meet with the leader of the American Gaean Commission," Marion said. "What was her name again?"

"Deirdre Tombs," Konig said. "We're going to meet with Deirdre Tombs."

THREE

Niflheimr's throne room had changed drastically in the last month, more so than any other part of the palace, thanks to Konig's mother. Violet had moved in during Marion's recovery and taken charge of decorating for the wedding. However, many of her touches were clearly meant to be permanent, from the tapestries of nymphs that concealed the cogs of ice to the furniture scattered around the nave.

The queen herself was seated upon the throne when Marion and Konig arrived. "You're late," Violet said.

"Barely." Deirdre Tombs offered a smile to Marion. "I'll forgive you for it this time, I guess."

The shifter leading the American Gaean Commission was startlingly young—which said a lot, considering Marion had yet to hit her twentieth birthday. Deirdre wore chunky combat boots, leather leggings, a leather jacket, and a tight leather corset. She looked like she should have been heading to a vampire bar for a night of bloodletting fun.

Deirdre jerked a thumb at the ornate chair Violet was sitting in. "Good move not doing another ice throne. I've got no idea what they were thinking the first time around, making a seat that melts."

Marion extended her hand to shake. "I'm so grateful that you were willing to have this conversation here. I know it's not convenient for gaeans to travel between the Middle Worlds."

"Really?" Deirdre looked at her hand, laughed, and pulled Marion into a hug.

"Oh," Marion said, surprised.

Deirdre looked just as surprised when she stepped back. "What's wrong?"

Marion hadn't inferred a friendship with Deirdre Tombs from reading her own journals, which had been written in a code that assigned obscure nicknames to everyone Marion knew. If they were friends, Marion surely would have written about it. She'd have to figure out what she had called Deirdre to know their history.

At least the AGC chair was greeting Marion with a hug instead of a gun.

"Wedding planning is overwhelming," Violet said when Marion failed to think of a response. "I'm afraid my future daughter-in-law has been distracted these past few weeks."

"Thanks for the help, Mother," Konig said pointedly.

Violet gave him a thin smile and finally stood.

The Onyx Queen was the obvious source of her son's otherworldly beauty. White hair flowed around a face shaped like his. Chains dangled from her tiara, just above the delicate bridge of her nose, and the fullness of her lips was the color of roses faded in sun.

When she slid down the steps from the throne, she was trailed by voluminous veils that made Marion's dress look like something she'd picked up at a gas station. It was the kind of descent that would have made anyone stop to stare. "Jolene Chang has already been released back to Earth," Violet said. "We couldn't allow her to stay. She wouldn't answer any of our questions."

Deirdre folded her arms. "What did you ask?"

"The wrong questions," Violet said. "If we'd asked the right things, we'd know why she was in the dungeons. Did you sanction her spying? Is that why you agreed to have this meeting in the Winter Court?"

"Mother," Konig snapped.

"It's a fair question," Deirdre said, lifting one shoulder in a shrug. "Jolene thinks she can find the darknet servers."

Heather had been right.

"Then you did sanction it," Violet said.

"No, I told her not to run off. If the darknet servers really are in the Winter Court, then they wouldn't be easily accessible from Niflheimr, and we're not in the habit of spying on allies," Deirdre said. "I'm sorry for Jolene's behavior. Thanks for taking it easy on her."

Violet inclined her head in graceful acceptance of the apology. "Then what do *you* want, Deirdre Tombs?"

"I was hoping I could just talk to Marion," Deirdre said. "Marion and Konig, if he's still speaker for the unseelie. And the talk should be alone, ideally."

"We aren't really speakers anymore," Marion said. "We only fulfilled those roles at the summit."

"You're both still authorized to make decisions for your factions, though," Deirdre said. "You know your favorite terrorist's gone legit, right?"

That was clearly a personal reference Marion should have understood. "Yes, I'm fully aware of your work with the American Gaean Commission. You're doing wonderful things."

Wonderful things, and dangerous things. Deirdre represented direct opposition to Rylie Gresham's institution. She'd also been gathering faction-free North American Union preternaturals at her back, forming something that resembled a rebellion, if not an overt army. She was chaos in shifter form, as far as the establishment was concerned, but she draped herself in the robes of justice. Democracy.

Deirdre presented a thick binder with "Proposal for International Preternatural Council" on the cover. "I want to make a permanent coalition out of the people who attended the summit. I think we can accomplish a lot of good for the world with ongoing cooperation. Here, look at this."

Marion took the binder and sat in one of the chairs on the floor of the throne room. It was the kind of furniture that Violet liked, all hand-carved wood and hard seats. She was forced to sit very straight or slide off onto the ground.

She flipped through the pages. It was a lot of information, but as a half-angel, Marion was capable of consuming staggering amounts of information in minimal time. Once she'd realized that she could speed-read at a rate of ten thousand words per minute with a little touch of angel magic, it had made tearing through her old journals a much easier chore.

Now she employed it to inhale Deirdre's proposal.

"It's good," Marion said, shutting the binder.

Amusement touched Deirdre's full lips. Amusement, but not surprise—she must have known Marion well indeed. "Gotta say, I'm relieved to have your approval. You're the linchpin."

"How so?" Konig asked.

"In the same way that she ensured the honesty of negotiations at the summit." Deirdre lifted her wrist to flash a bracelet identical to the one that Marion had used on Geoff Samuelson.

Marion relaxed a tiny amount—as much as she could while sitting in one of Violet's stiff chairs. The bracelet's compulsion meant Deirdre couldn't lie. When she said that she wanted to use the group to benefit the world, she must have been honest about the good intentions.

"We've also adapted the magically binding contract you wrote up for the summit to create a new contract for this council," Deirdre said. "I've got copies both of you can check out. All the other factions have already signed on, including Adàn Pedregon, and he's a real pain in the ass."

She took a pair of envelopes from her bag, handing one to Marion and then climbing the stairs to give the other to Konig. He'd sat on the throne that his mother had vacated. His lazy rockstar posture, and the fact that Violet had returned to tower at his side, made him look a little too sullen to be king.

"Here's the proposal for those who can't read *War and Peace* in a half-hour. Each speaker agrees to contribute to a system of checks and balances for the factions. When we vote on something, the vote's binding, magical-style. If we all vote to say that it's illegal for sidhe to eat cupcakes, we've all gotta enforce that."

"I'm not voting against cupcakes," Marion said.

"Just an example," Deirdre said. "Full disclosure, motivated by my fancy-shiny bracelet: the voting body will also be capable of removing people from power. If Rylie Gresham goes nuts, we'll be able to vote a new Alpha in without a nationwide election."

Violet peered over her son's shoulder at the contract. "This sounds unconscionably intrusive."

"It's a safety net meant to take overwhelming power from any one faction."

"It's undemocratic to take leadership choices away from the people," Marion said.

Deirdre smiled at Marion. "The Alpha only became an electable position because Rylie wanted it that way, so she's still got absolute power. Without this agreement, she can change her mind about holding elections at all."

"This would impact the sidhe royal families." Violet plucked the contract out of Konig's hands.

He took it back. "Stop, Mother. This is my choice. You made me speaker for the unseelie. And I have to say, Deirdre, I'm intrigued."

"You should be. This could save lives. A lot of lives." Deirdre planted her hands on her hips. "Look, Genesis screwed everything up, big time. And you know what caused that?"

"The gods dicking around with reality?" Konig suggested.

"Pre-Genesis factions pissing off the gods. The angels were getting all up in everyone's business, and the demons pulled the Breaking thing, and it was a mess. Rebooting the universe was the gods' solution to cleaning it up. We're lucky we didn't get forty days and nights of rain too."

"You want to be able to have all of the factions magically bound together to prevent another Genesis," Marion said.

"Exactly," Deirdre said. "We'll only vote on big stuff like that. It takes ten of the twelve factions agreeing we need a vote in order to do it. Although we can also chat more casually about other stuff—open up more diplomatic relations and stuff."

Marion skimmed her copy of the contract. It was bordered with ethereal runes like those she had all over spell books in her private home, back on Vancouver Island. She traced her fingertips along the runes as the internet guides to magic had instructed. The spells whispered their truths to her.

Despite the simple designs, the magic behind them was immense. The elegance and complexity were breathtaking. Marion had a hard time imagining she'd ever been able to craft such a thing even though her fingerprints were all over it. The spells practically sang in delight at her acknowledgment.

It would be easy enough to activate the runes in the master contract. Marion could definitely bind the council.

"This cannot go through," Violet said.

"It's not your decision," Deirdre said. "Right, Prince ErlKonig?"

He puffed up at being addressed directly. "Right."

"I like the idea," Marion said. The last thing they needed was another Genesis, and the gods had made it clear they weren't afraid of interfering when people made them angry. "I have to wonder, though—what's the specific motivation behind getting this together now?"

"It was inspired by events at the summit," Deirdre said promptly. "We've got to be able to unite against threats—like demons—that might motivate another god-driven catastrophe."

She set the master contract out on a marble-topped table and produced a pen.

Ten of twelve factions had signed it.

"I'm amazed you got everyone to cooperate." Marion had barely survived the week of the summit without punching anyone in the nose, and she wasn't the nose-punching type.

"You're not the only one who's good at politics," Deirdre said. "Plus the whole 'I can set fire to anyone who pisses me off' thing doesn't hurt."

Marion's eyes widened. She'd been told Deirdre Tombs was a shapeshifter. What kind of shifter could set fire to people?

Deirdre misinterpreted her reaction. "I'm kidding. I've spent weeks talking people into it. Cupcakes might have been involved—not cupcakes I made, mind you, because I'm awful at baking. *Good* cupcakes."

"You didn't bring any for me?"

"I didn't think they'd last the trip between worlds. I'll give you an IOU if you sign." She offered the pen to Marion. "All my work to this point means nothing if you and your husband-to-be don't join the group."

Violet ripped the pen out of Deirdre's hand. "Where were you, Deirdre Tombs, when the sidhe courts needed to be established? What did you sacrifice to establish benevolent monarchies that would care for the sidhe when nobody else did?"

Deirdre didn't even blink. "I was getting shuttled between orphanages because Genesis killed my dad and left me without a home."

Konig sauntered down the stairs and took the pen from his mother. "I'll sign, and you will too, Marion."

"You're making a grave mistake," Violet said.

Her son had already signed.

Now he extended the pen to Marion. "Do it, princess."

Deirdre was practically glowing as Marion signed. "Now you just have to activate it," the shifter said. "Go ahead."

Marion stroked the page. She felt the instant that the binding spell activated. It locked into her breastbone like an invisible golden chain.

For a moment, the pain was so immense that she couldn't breathe.

It was gone as quickly.

"Thanks." Deirdre folded the contract and tucked it into her bag again. "I look forward to seeing you guys at the vote next week."

Marion blinked. "Next week?"

"We're voting to have Konig's title as Prince of the Autumn Court removed. He won't be heir. He won't hold lands. That way, if the two of you get married, the peace treaty with the angels still won't extend to the Winter Court." Deirdre's shrug almost looked embarrassed. "Sorry."

"But...but..." Marion's mouth opened and closed. The only thing she managed to get out was, "You're wearing the bracelet."

"I told you nothing but the truth, so help me gods. The voting body is meant to prevent god-level disasters again. And like you told us at the summit, Marion: the gods will have blood if you let the angels have the Winter Court." Fierce light filled Deirdre's eyes. "I'm not going to let that happen."

"That's not what we're planning to do." Marion would never dream of giving the Winter Court to the angels since Leliel killed the refugees.

"But you *could* do it," Deirdre said. "Just like how Rylie doesn't have to have elections for Alpha because she's got absolute power. Nobody can have absolute power to ruin the world—even you, Marion."

Shimmering magic overcame Konig. Niflheimr trembled with his fury. "I signed your contract!"

Marion felt dizzy. *Ten of twelve people are needed to call a vote.*

Everyone Deirdre had spoken to had agreed that Konig needed to be removed as prince.

Everyone she had worked with at the summit.

"Get her!" Violet roared, thrusting a finger toward the shifter.

The Raven Knights materialized from the ley lines. Even Marion, mostly immune to the reality distortion effects of sidhe magic, found herself incapable of standing when they swarmed in with battle magic flaring. She lost all sense of body. Her eyes and ears overloaded, reducing Niflheimr to fuzzy whiteness.

She could still see enough to know that

Deirdre shifted in a burst of flame. The AGC chair became a firebird—something halfway between heron and hawk, assuming she'd been rolled in kerosene then shot through a bonfire via cannon.

Deirdre seized the bag with the contract in massive talons and vanished into the night, untouched.

"So much for cupcakes," Marion said faintly.

FOUR

New York City, New York—January 2031

A bar called Rock Bottom should have been an ironic hangout for rich kids pretending to be poor, but there was nothing ironic about the lightless dive squeezed into the basement of a bodega. Its dirt-caked windows were tired eyes gazing across cracked sidewalks, while its shadowy interior was its rotten brain filled with the sick thoughts that were its patrons.

Not ironic, but honest. Refreshing in a way. But mostly depressing because Seth Wilder fit the name perfectly.

Sunlight burned a square onto the dusty floor when he opened the door to step inside. Mutters of protest broke through the crowd, like it was strange to open that front door during daytime. The dozens of patrons must have never left.

He walked past the bar and all the pixie liquor, which held no allure for him at the moment. He ignored the naked woman with a tattooed venus mound offering cubes of lethe with blood-caked fingers. He also ignored the gang of vampires blowing clouds of hookah into one another's faces, but ignoring the vampires was the hardest.

All the lives in the bar demanded his attention. What they were now, with pallid faces and desperate fingers, was only a small part of it. Their entire lives cried out to Seth: from the moment each individual had been birthed from the waters of the womb forward into inevitably grave futures. The grave times were brightest for Seth, where his heart wanted to be.

Everyone should have had their graves in the future.

Vampires didn't.

They hadn't been birthed from flesh, but from dirt. Their bloodless bodies craved fuel to power them a few more days into defiant undeath.

The strongest of the undead was waiting for him at a table in the back.

Lucifer was watching the news on an old pre-Genesis CRT television. It teetered on a wobbly table by his side, its power cables running under his feet.

"You're late." Lucifer turned down the volume. He was a whip-lean vampire with slicked hair and a cadaverous pallor. He didn't glisten anything like the powerful sidhe, or even the colorless beauty of a half-incubus Gray.

He was dead, and he'd been dead for years.

Lucifer had acted as speaker for the vampires during the recent preternatural summit held at the United Nations. How he had ended up speaker was hard to pinpoint. Vampires were very loosely affiliated. More of them aligned with Deirdre Tombs's American Gaean Commission than Lucifer's people. Yet he'd had enough authority to show up at the summit.

Somehow, Lucifer was more than the usual petty drug lord feeding off the worst of preternatural society. And Seth needed him.

Lucifer gestured to the chair opposite his. "Hold tight. I'll be with you in a second." He was watching the news while January Lazar, celebrity newscaster who'd made her fame profiling important preternaturals, reported on increasing demonic possessions nationwide.

"You know anything about what's happening with that?" Seth asked.

"I wouldn't tell you for free if I did." Lucifer's crimson eyes finally weighed on him. "Don't tell me what you want. Let me guess. I'm sure you're not here for my drugs."

"That's right. I'm not."

"Shut up, I told you not to tell me." Lucifer drummed his fingers on his thigh. "You're a nice guy, so you don't want me to knock someone off. You don't want power because you've clearly got enough of that. I've only got two guesses: either you want me to hide you, or you're looking for someone."

"Can I tell you now?" Seth asked. Lucifer nodded. "I need black-market magic. Something that will keep me alive."

"Shoot, I thought I was good at guessing." The vampire reclined in his chair, arms folded behind his head. "You're coming to a dead man for eternal life even though you already have eternal youth. What are you?"

Seth's eyes flicked around the bar. There were no familiar faces—no Dana McIntyre—but that didn't mean there were no triadists who might recognize him for what he was. Lives and deaths whirled around him in dizzying variety.

"I'm human," Seth said.

"Not exactly."

"No," he admitted reluctantly. "Not exactly. I'm human enough that I can die and I don't want that to happen."

"What walks on two legs, is 'human enough' to die, but eternally young?"

"How do you know about the..." Seth lowered his voice. "The eternal youth."

"I'm a vampire," Lucifer said. "I know what it looks like on a man. So tell me, old guy—what have you got hiding under that shirt of yours?"

Seth glanced down at his shirt. There was nothing to see except cotton. What had given away his injury? Did vampires have acute smell like werewolves did? "All I'm packing is chest stubble. I missed my last appointment with the Bic."

"Show me."

"Screw you."

"Show me or you're leaving here with nothing."

"I doubt you have anything."

"I do," Lucifer said. "I've got the secret to life. You won't find out unless you flash me."

Seth clenched his jaw, grabbed the hem of his shirt, and lifted.

He didn't look down at himself again. He'd spent enough time staring through a motel's cracked bathroom mirror to have memorized the mire of glistening organs exposed by his chest wound. He'd been torn apart by Arawn's Hounds in Sheol and wasn't healing. It wasn't like the time he'd been stabbed by a sidhe assassin protecting Marion. He'd walked it off after a touch of TLC and a bottle of whiskey.

This wound was permanent. Worse, it had been degrading over the last few weeks.

The cage of Seth's tooth-scraped ribs held light captive, tangled up with his intestines. The pulse of his heart forced unnatural energy like a lightning-ripped storm through his body. Every beat made his skin flake a little more.

Seth wasn't dying from the wound. He was dying from whatever was trapped inside of his mortal body. If what followed his death was what Dana McIntyre claimed, he wasn't ready to face it.

"Happy?" Seth asked, dropping the shirt.

"That's not a word in my vocabulary," Lucifer said. "Let's talk immortality."

"Vampires weren't around before Genesis.

Staying twenty-five years old for fifteen years doesn't make you an expert in immortality."

"There were immortals before Genesis. Eons-old angels and demons." Lucifer's dark eyes gleamed. "There were gods, too."

"Are you a triadist?"

"I know a few of them."

"Are any of them named Dana McIntyre or Oliver Machado?" Either would have meant Seth needed to beat a quick exit.

The pause before Lucifer responded meant that he had no clue who those people were. "I don't divulge the names of contacts."

"People divulge your name," Seth said. "You get talked about a lot in bad circles. You're supposed to work the worst kind of miracles. If anyone can make someone—something—like me stay alive, you'll know about it."

Lucifer lifted a finger to quiet him. "Wait." The news had come back from commercial break. January Lazar was talking again.

"I don't have all day."

"We just established that you have eternity," Lucifer said. "*Wait.*" The vampire stared intently at the news anchor. There were no subtitles, and the audio was quiet enough that Seth couldn't hear it, but Lucifer must have been getting something out of it.

Or else he just liked annoying Seth.

Without shifting his eyes from the television, Lucifer said, "You're a demon. I feel it all over you."

"I'm not," Seth said.

"Infernal. You're drenched in infernal energy. Preternaturals, we're all a family, even between factions—some of us more closely related than others. Shifters are closer to sidhe. Sidhe are closer to angels. And vampires are closer to demons."

The door to the bar opened, allowing harsh daylight to spill through Rock Bottom. Protesting voices lifted in shouts again.

Someone had come inside. It was impossible to see who it was at that distance. Seth doubted it was Dana McIntyre, but the mere possibility of it had him on edge. "Get to the point."

"Vampires are just this side of infernal," Lucifer reiterated. "You'll need to feed the way we do if you want to heal your body. I can hook you up with blood."

The revulsion was immediate and overwhelming. "No."

He'd spent years fighting to ignore his visceral reaction to spilled blood. Working as a doctor, the battle had been relentless—what a revenant friend of his called living in the eye of the storm. Always an inch from getting ripped apart by hurricane winds.

Seth had strayed an inch too far from the eye of the storm in Sheol. He'd fed on Marion and still remembered the sweetness of death in her blood.

He would never do that again.

"Blood or meat, pick your poison," Lucifer said. "Demons tend to go for meat over blood because it's more substantial, but blood should do the trick. Bonus: it's less likely to be fatal to your victims."

"*No*," Seth said again. "I can't do either."

"You can if you want to fix...that." He flicked his fingers at Seth's shirt.

The cloth was loose enough that it didn't suck into the cavity of Seth's body. But it fell over his exposed ribs when he wasn't careful. And he wasn't being careful now. When Seth finally dared to look down, he could see the outline of bones. "There has to be another option."

"Blood can be extracted without murder. If that doesn't work—if you need meat—then I can help you with that, too. Vampires aren't bad people. I can tell you what we do to target the dregs of society nobody will miss."

The dregs of society that Seth had healed in his hospital.

There was no such thing as a person nobody would miss. Everyone mattered. Everyone was important.

"Thanks for your time," Seth said, standing up.

Lucifer watched him stand with obvious irritation. "You wanted a deal with the devil."

"I've made such deals before," he said. "I always regretted it."

"The devil's your last choice."

"Second to last." If he couldn't bring himself to deal with vampires, he could still turn to an angel for help. A specific half-angel who he would have preferred not to risk seeing again, even though he desperately missed her.

"There's one other thing we could do for each other. If you're 'human enough,' I can take the 'enough' part away." Lucifer tongued his incisors, which weren't much sharper than an ordinary man's. "I'll make you a vampire."

The idea was only two degrees less revolting than being a demon. But vampires could survive on synthetic blood, and Seth couldn't at the moment—he'd already tried that.

He sat back down. "All right. We can talk."

"You need to do something for me before I'll change you," Lucifer said.

"I told you, no deals with the devil. If you're attaching strings then I'll just ask another vampire to do it." Someone like Charity Ballard, a revenant who would happily help Seth. He'd been avoiding her for as long as he'd avoided Marion, but it would be easy enough to track the thread of her life once he was ready.

"I'm the only devil you'll find who can do this. Few vampires have the strength to make others." Lucifer smirked, as if he knew what Seth was thinking. "And not all breeds can change others."

Most likely revenants among them.

Seth's eyebrows lowered. "All right. What would you want?"

"Root access to the darknet servers. They're in the Winter Court and I saw you at the summit with the steward. You two are clearly intimate. Have her give you access."

Marion probably didn't know how to get in,

SM Reine

either, but it would be an excuse to visit with her, and he wanted to visit. Badly. It was a drive both alluring and dangerous. "So you want root access. That means a login that lets you administrate the servers. Why?"

"I'm a businessman and all the good business happens on the darknet. I want to be in charge of that."

"I'll think about it." Seth would have to think a lot longer and harder about whether he wanted to be a vampire than the darknet issue, though.

Before he could leave, a familiar face on Lucifer's television caught his attention.

The news stories had switched over. Now January Lazar was talking about a young woman with heart-shaped features and hair the same shade as soil after rainfall. She was dusky in coloring, her flesh a shade too dark to be Mediterranean olive, her eyebrows strong and straight and almost angry-looking. That was what made the contrast of her white-blue eyes so shocking.

Marion Garin stood beside a second familiar face, which Seth found less appealing. Prince ErlKonig of the Autumn Court had an especially irritating smile in the footage that January Lazar was talking over. The two of them were in Hollywood, walking from a limousine to a theater.

Marion had a way of moving that made it look like she had wings, even though no such thing was visible at her back.

"What's happening there?" Seth asked.

"The Voice of God has confirmed that she's getting married to the unseelie Prince of the Autumn Court in a week," Lucifer said. "They sent out invitations a few days ago and someone leaked it to the news."

Married.

For a dizzying moment, Seth wasn't surrounded by vampires in Rock Bottom anymore.

He was a younger man waiting at the altar for a beautiful blond werewolf Alpha. She had been pregnant at the time. Seth had believed that the babies, the twins, belonged to him.

It had been a snowy day when he'd been due to marry Rylie Gresham. And it hadn't happened. Enemies had attacked their wedding before vows could be exchanged, blood had been spilled across the snow, and the nuptials had been interrupted.

Then he had learned that the babies weren't even his.

Everything had fallen apart after that.

Twenty years later, he was alone. Rylie was still running the largest werewolf pack in the world alongside Seth's brother, Abel—the father of her children. Her werewolf Alpha mate.

It still hurt.

Seth had promised himself never to deal with that hurt again.

He had sworn to be forever alone with that pain, letting old wounds heal, forgotten, while he dealt with a life beyond love.

That pain had nothing to do with Marion's wedding to Konig.

Nothing at all.

Yet the giant hole in his chest was hurting more than it had since he'd been eaten by the Hounds.

FIVE

"We'll assassinate her," Konig said. "Assassinate, dismember, and display her head atop the walls of Myrkheimr. I'll see her skewered for this!"

Marion reclined on the throne, massaging her temples to relax the headache holding her skull in a vise. It had started with the Raven Knights' unsuccessful attempt to seize Deirdre, but it continued because Konig had been ranting about murder for the last hour.

Jibril's arrival hadn't helped assuage his temper, either. The normally calm angel was only feeding into Konig's fire.

"You might have to settle for a less-favored appendage," Jibril said. "I want her head on a pike in Dilmun." That was the angel city in the Ethereal Levant. Marion had only ever seen it through Leliel's memories, but if it was head-on-a-pike territory, she didn't want to visit in person.

"We could bisect her head and each take half," Konig suggested.

Marion rolled her eyes. "You can't kill a phoenix." Violet had explained Deirdre's nature as soon as the shifter had departed.

"Actually, you can," Heather said. She'd been summoned by Konig's rage along with the Knights, and now she was skinning the dead Hound at the end of the hall. "A phoenix is rumored to be easier to kill than other shifters. The problem is that they have a nasty habit of coming back sooner or later."

"Even coming back 'later' would be preferable to having her strip my title," Konig snarled. "She only needs to be dead until the vote!"

Violet didn't say anything, but the magic shimmering over her porcelain skin was distinctly smug. The fact that she'd resisted saying "I told you so" was even more miraculous than a phoenix shifter's ability to be reborn from death.

"We can't assassinate Deirdre," Marion said, more firmly the second time.

"Heather can arrange it," Konig said.

"It's true, I can," Heather agreed.

Marion lifted her head from her hands. "We won't kill Deirdre over this—not least of all because it would be ineffective. She'd just be replaced by Jolene." Jolene liked Marion as little as anyone else that she'd encountered. Worse, Jolene was, despite being described as "good people," the kind of person who sneaked into the Niflheimr dungeons in search of the darknet.

"I won't give up my title," Konig said.

"You won't need to," Marion said. "We can lobby for votes the way that Deirdre will."

"Let me remind you that ten of twelve of your ilk already think that Konig's position as prince is something that should be voted upon," Violet said. "The odds are hardly in your favor."

"I can't believe you signed such a thing on behalf of the angels without first consulting me," Jibril said, turning his anger on Marion now. She was a much more convenient target than Deirdre.

"Blame Leliel," Marion said. "She's the one who made me speaker."

Jibril pulled his wings tightly against his back. "Oh, I do blame Leliel. I blame her for a great many things." The angels had been quick to disassociate themselves from Leliel's attack on the Winter Court. Leliel was leader in the EL, and that leadership came with power, just as Marion's stewardship came with ties to Niflheimr. It didn't necessarily come with loyalty.

Jibril had been in the throne room almost daily to foster goodwill. He'd all but kissed Konig's feet to avoid the wrath of the sidhe. No actual foot-kissing had happened, but Jibril had agreed to perform Konig and Marion's wedding ceremony in a public display of peace.

"I won't be bullied," Konig said. "Especially not in regards to something so important to me." He took Marion's hand, brushing his lips over the knuckles. It reminded her of their long day in bed together. The mere memory of it weakened her knees. "We need to have Deirdre Tombs killed."

Marion used his hand to help her stand from the throne. "We must do this the right way. I have connections among every faction—even if I don't remember them. I'll pull strings and convince everyone to vote in our favor."

"I don't know if that's the better outcome," the angel said. "What if Deirdre Tombs is right? What if your marriage makes the gods angry? What if this leads to another Genesis-like event?"

"We can risk gods who are meant to love me destroying the world over my wedding," Marion said, "or we can be sure that the Winter Court will fall, and there won't be anything to keep Leliel from killing us all. One is a gamble and one is a guarantee."

"Lobbying for votes among factions who hate you is a hell of a gamble too, princess," Konig said.

It was the truth, but it still stung. "We don't have to be likable. We have to be compelling."

Violet smiled bitterly. It looked especially vacant with her whited-out eyes. "In that case, I suppose I should get back to planning your wedding."

Before entering the weeks-long recovery that had followed bleeding into the soul links, Marion had made a few important wedding decisions. She'd explored Niflheimr for a location that was structurally safe, relatively warm, and distant from the carnage that Leliel had wreaked upon the courtyard. Marion had found a chamber in one of the towers adjacent that met all requirements perfectly.

Whatever role the room had served before the revolution, nobody seemed to know. It was vast and empty and connected to the visitors' bedrooms by a hallway. Privately, Marion suspected the Winter Court had used it for orgies. The sidhe liked to use everything for orgies.

Violet had needed Marion's permission to make substantial changes to Niflheimr, but a few drops of blood later, the chamber had yielded control to the visiting queen. She'd managed to make things grow in the ice. Trees. Vines. Even furniture. The mere presence of flora seemed to have brought humidity with it, and dampness clung to every corner.

After Jibril left, Violet threw herself back into the magical labor of modifying the wedding venue. Nori was helping—or so she claimed. For the time being, helping seemed to be following Violet around and keeping track of her executive decisions so she'd be able to update the happy couple on what was transpiring.

Marion watched with reluctant amusement, hanging back where several benches were stacked in a pile. She knew better than to get involved when Violet was urging the ice to turn into perpetual waterfalls flanking the altar where the vows would be exchanged.

"You can't fault your mother for her vision," Marion said, trying to force a smile for Konig. The trees shivered as he stalked toward her. Sidhe didn't skimp on sex, and they didn't skimp on temper tantrums, either.

"Maybe Deirdre Tombs is right," Konig said. "Maybe our marriage is damned by the gods."

Marion glanced at Violet, who was conducting more seats to grow from the floor near the front of the room. They were like wooden vines wrapping together, forming into the shape of seats more perfectly than any careful hand-carving could have.

She drew Konig further away, just in case his mother was listening.

"You don't need to be afraid of losing your title as prince," Marion whispered. "We won't let it happen."

"I'm not afraid of anything! But you must realize that we can't leverage your relationships to lobby for votes. The wards on Niflheimr are already weak. If you keep leaving the plane to talk to people..."

"I'll strengthen the soul links as many times as I need to. I'm feeling much better. I can spill a lot of blood again."

"And need a wheelchair to attend your wedding?" He snorted. "That's going to look fantastic on the cover of *Vogue*."

"I won't need to drain myself as much this time. We're just a few days from the wedding."

Once Konig was married to the Winter Court's steward, assuming the role of king, he'd be able to connect to the sidhe magic. He'd be able to recast everything. The wards would be strong, and neither of them would need to suffer major blood loss over it.

"If there will be any wedding at all," Konig said.

"Are you reconsidering the wedding?"

"Not because of *her*, and what she might do to me. Because of what she said about the gods. Just because she's an asshole doesn't mean she isn't also right. How do we know that this won't make the gods come slamming down on us? When's the last time you even talked to them?"

Marion could remember the exact moment she spoke to them—one of them, anyway. "When Seth brought me back here after Sheol. When he was in my bedroom."

"You talked to the gods after that?"

"No, I talked to Seth when he was in my room." She drew in a breath, clenched her fists, squared her shoulders. "Everything with the Canope was set up to force Seth to reveal himself as a god. I'm sorry I didn't tell you sooner, but it wasn't my secret to tell."

"Are you sure?" Konig asked. "You're absolutely certain he's a god?"

"I'd be the one who knows, wouldn't I?"

She'd expected him to be angry that she waited so long to tell him. Instead, he looked relieved. "We've got a god on our side. An actual god! I knew I liked Seth for a reason." Marion was confident that Konig hadn't liked Seth until that moment. "That means we have another strategy for getting votes that doesn't require you to leave Niflheimr unprotected!"

"We do?"

He was getting excited now. "What do you think Deirdre Tombs told ten preternatural leaders to convince them to this degree of control? She said this would protect them from the gods, and you're not on the gods' side anymore. But we've got one of them. We can prove her wrong."

"He wouldn't want everyone to know about him, Konig. He chose to live as a doctor for a reason."

"He's going to save us," Konig said. It was like he'd gone deaf. "We should tell everyone. They'll bend to us immediately."

"No," Marion said, appalled. "Don't you realize how many people would blame him for Genesis? Please, Konig. Promise you'll keep it a secret."

His face fell. "Marion..."

"*Please.*"

"Only for you. Anything for you." He kissed her temple. "I didn't get a chance to ask you how things went with Geoff Samuelson."

"Confusingly. He told me that the person who attacked me outside Original Sin was—okay, this will sound crazy. She had the head of a goat."

"I don't suppose your sister was fathered by a goat?"

Marion laughed. "No. It's not my sister."

"You must be relieved."

Relieved wasn't a strong enough word for it. Learning that her deity half-sister was out to get her would have been a much bigger problem than the one posed by Deirdre Tombs. "It's confusing, as I said. Have you ever heard of a creature with the body of a person and the head of a goat?"

"I haven't, but you might have a way to figure it out." A sly smile crept across his lips. "If you were to lobby for votes, your first stop would be Rylie Gresham, wouldn't it?"

"I hadn't thought that far."

"She'll have computers with access to the OPA databases. Everything that they know can be searched through that. I'm certain that they've seen people with goat heads, if anyone has."

It wasn't a terrible idea, though it did have one major flaw. "I don't know Rylie well enough to trust her with this information. Until I know who the goat-woman is and what, exactly, she did to me... I still don't know who's connected." She twined her fingers through Konig's. "You're the only one I can trust with this information."

His eyes warmed at that, and he squeezed her hand tightly.

The words he spoke next weren't as warm. "Then don't tell her about it. Just use her computer." He brushed a kiss over her cheek, barely touching the corner of her lips. And then he went to Nori and Violet to help grow more trees for their wedding.

Gods. Marion's wedding. She was going to be

married within days, and she was going to have to spend that time running around lobbying for votes.

To think Violet had told her those would be the happiest days of her life.

"The ceremony will occur here," Violet said, lifting both hands in tandem. A new tree rose between the twin waterfalls. "You'll stand here, and Marion will stand there." Another gesture, and the icy floor turned to grass budding with flowers. "What do you think?"

It had been so long since she'd asked for Konig's opinion that he didn't realize she'd spoken to him. He was distracted by watching Marion glide out of the hall, a slender form whose gown was a crimson mirror of her chestnut hair. Marion was beautiful enough to be sidhe, but so much more special.

A god. She'd brought a *god* into their partnership.

Konig had hoped she would, of course. But before her memory loss, she had repeatedly refused to use her privileges as the Voice of God with anything related to Konig.

No longer.

The doctor Marion liked to pal around with was one of the gods, so her value had just increased exponentially. Impressive, considering that she was already priceless.

"What do you think?" His mother asked the question louder the second time.

"Hmm?"

"Oh, darling." Violet cupped his cheek in her hand, blank eyes warming with genuine affection. "Transfixed by your bride, are you?" Even Violet, who had never been fond of Marion, appreciated what she perceived as desire between the two of them.

"She's quite a prize," Konig said.

Nori didn't look at either of them. "I like the waterfalls," she said, bustling around the new tree with a strand of witchlights. They'd be twined through all the branches to provide an unearthly glow to the ceremony.

"I didn't ask you." Violet turned back to her work on the hall. "I shouldn't bother asking my boy, either. Boys never care about these things. You've much more important things to consider." She cast loops of magic toward the roof, peppering it with blossoms of starlight.

"More important than my wedding?" Konig asked.

"Actually, we do have some important court business to talk about, if the queen doesn't need us anymore," Nori said. She tucked the last of the witchlights among the tree branches.

Violet dismissed them with another flick of her fingers. "Attend to the court."

As if Konig needed her permission.

Much as it rankled to leave his mother in

charge of anything, he really didn't care about how things looked during the ceremony. And as long as she was busy with decorations, she wouldn't be sitting on the throne. The woman was practically dancing on the bones of the Winter Queen.

Nori kept her head bowed as she led Konig from the hall, back toward the king's bedroom. The hall was so much chillier that Konig couldn't help but suck in a breath. He kept forgetting where they were.

But his blood burned hot enough to keep him warm.

As soon as the doors to the wedding venue swung shut behind him, he caught Nori's wrist. "Court business?" he murmured, pulling her to his chest.

Spots of pink touched her cheeks. "Very important court business."

Konig's fingers glided up her ribcage. "Tell me all about it."

"It's Ymir," Nori said.

That chilled his desire. "Again? Damn. Where is he?"

"I had him brought to our room by the Raven Knights." Nori ducked her head, but not before Konig saw her flushing even brighter with embarrassment. "*Your* room."

It was an easy slip to make. Nori had been spending more nights in his bed than anywhere else. The succor of her half-angel flesh was the only thing keeping Konig sane while he waited for

Marion's frigidity to thaw.

Two of the Raven Knights were guarding the door to the king's bedroom. Konig made a mental note to have more assigned on that hall. With Arawn throwing Hounds at their doorstep, nothing was more important than ensuring Konig's safety.

He was only days away from being king. *Days.* Konig would not let an uppity demon interfere with that.

Ymir waited inside the room, watched by yet another pair of Raven Knights wearing warm furred coats. The frost giant wore a t-shirt and jeans instead. Ymir seemed to find temperatures in the palace summer-like.

The child was munching on a candy bar—not his first, judging by the many wrappers around him. He looked as content as he ever did these days.

Every scrap of momentary contentment vanished when Konig strode into the room.

Ymir bolted to his feet. A strangled groan caught in the boy's chest.

"You're right," Konig said. "This *is* urgent." The frost giant shouldn't have been able to vocalize through the force of Konig's magic in his chest. Such groans meant he was shaking the magic again. It wouldn't be long before he was outright talking.

And once he started talking, Ymir would tell Marion that it hadn't been Leliel who killed the refugees.

"Come here," Konig said with all the kindness he could muster. He sat the boy on the couch and took the spot beside him.

Ymir managed to say something that sounded like, "No."

Konig swirled fresh magic around Ymir—stronger this time. The child didn't make another sound.

"There," Konig said, patting him on the back. "This won't be necessary soon, I promise. I just need to be sure that you don't go around spreading confusing lies about the attack you saw from an angel. I've got a very important day coming up, after all."

Marion had only agreed to give Konig another chance because she thought the angels were a threat. If she heard Ymir's side of things—and if she found out that Konig had lied to her—then their wedding would be wrecked.

"Why don't you find somewhere for the boy to play that's safer?" Konig asked the Raven Knights. "There are a lot of holes in this part of the palace. Take him down deep and make sure he can have fun where he won't get hurt."

Ymir was still shaking his head when they led him out of the room.

Konig and Nori were alone.

"That was close," she said. "I think he was trying to find Marion to talk to her earlier."

"It won't be a problem." Konig drew the half-angel into his lap, settling back to allow her to sit comfortably atop him. Nori wasn't as beautiful as

Marion, but at least she had many things in common with Konig. Like priorities. And a fondness for sex that Marion used to have, back when she'd been herself.

He allowed her to kiss him for a moment before drawing back. "This will have to wait, pet. I need you to do another kind of favor for me."

"If it involves Violet, I'm not sure she'll tolerate my presence much longer."

"Then you'll be happy to know this involves leaving Niflheimr." He slid his hand into her furs, seeking the contact of warm woman-flesh against his fingertips. "I need you to dig up everything you can find on Deirdre Tombs. We need leverage against her in case our other bid for votes fails."

"No problem." Nori shook her furs to the floor to expose her lean body. Even if she wasn't a particularly beautiful half-angel, she was still very much a half-angel, and that meant the statuesque elegance that came with it. "But what if there's nothing to dig up?"

Assassination was on the table. "I will not lose my title," Konig said, kissing Nori's throat. "And the wedding *will* happen."

Marion used the magic mirror in the throne room to arrange her hair while it was still reflective. Most likely it was sacrilege to use such a rare artifact for purposes of vanity, but it wasn't like she could make business calls rumpled from traveling between planes.

A figure appeared behind her in the reflection.

"Your Highness? Do you have a moment?"

She turned to greet Morrighan, one of the sidhe refugees. "Of course I do." For the people whose families she'd failed to protect, she had infinite time.

Morrighan approached the throne hesitantly. She was one of the gentry but shone with enough blue light that she would have needed to work to conceal her magical nature. "I was a witch who specialized in wards before Genesis. As a result, my sidhe talent is likewise ward specialization, and I've been feeling disruptions in Niflheimr for weeks."

"Yes, I understand that the wards are failing," Marion said. "Please don't worry yourself about them. We have a plan."

"That's not what I mean. Someone seems to be testing the wards regularly to see if they're still up, like calling a phone to see if anyone answers and then immediately hanging up."

Prickles spread down the back of Marion's neck. "Can you tell who?"

"It's strong," Morrighan said. "Other than that, I don't know."

It must have been Arawn—or perhaps even someone from the American Gaean Commission waiting for a chance to invade over the darknet.

The information didn't change anything. They still needed to repair the wards as quickly as possible.

Marion would see if she could double the number of Raven Knights on the castle in the meantime.

"Thank you for warning me," she said. "How have you been faring?"

Morrighan gave her a blank look. "How do you think?"

"Yes, I suppose that's a foolish question." Marion swallowed down apologies that would have been hollow. No words could return to Morrighan what had been lost.

"Rhiannon's all I have left now," Morrighan said. "The court doesn't even look how it used to anymore." She gazed at the Onyx Queen's nymph tapestries with obvious loathing.

"I thought you came from Leiptr."

"I fled to the forests after the civil war to survive. Anyone who didn't leave Niflheimr died."

But she had once attended court with the Winter Queen. Now she *really* had Marion's attention. "Do you know anything of the darknet servers?"

"That was Hardwick territory," Morrighan said. "They didn't let anyone else interfere with it."

"Hardwick?"

"Pierce and Jaycee Hardwick, two of the queen's dearest advisors. They were secretive types. I knew that they were running the darknet from the Winter Court, but not from where. Nobody but them had access."

"Tell me, Morrighan," Marion said, "if

someone were to search for the servers, where would you start?"

"I'd start by going back ten years and asking the Hardwicks. You'd never find the servers without them." Morrighan turned to leave the throne room, the glow of the magic mirror reflecting off her shiny brown hair. "You could always investigate their bedrooms, though."

Marion wanted to follow her and ask for more information, but the mirror's glow intensified. She was being connected with the shapeshifter sanctuary. Her time to give a neglected refugee attention had passed because it was time for business.

It was *always* time for business.

Once Marion came to terms with the fact that her life didn't belong to her, she would be a much happier woman.

SIX

The next day, Nori took Marion to the designated arrival point outside the werewolf sanctuary's wards, which was near the top of the waterfall. From that vantage point, Marion could see everything: the jagged lines of the valley carved into the Appalachians, forest so dense that it must have been eternal night under the canopy, the lake frothing gold with reflected sunlight.

At the nadir of the valley sprawled the sanctuary's cottages ringing a humble downtown unlike any other in North America. It was the only settlement that exclusively housed preternaturals —and more than ninety-eight percent of them shapeshifters. Eighty percent of those were werewolves, like the Alpha and her mate.

For every summer when Marion had been a child, there had also been one half-angel mage who lived there. According to her journals, she used to play with the Alpha's kids for days on end.

"Ringing any bells?" Nori asked.

Marion was forced to say, "Not really."

An escort of shifters emerged from the forest. They resembled mundane wolves because they had four legs, fur, and lupine faces. But their sheer size would have given them away as something different. Something *wrong*. None of them was smaller than a very sturdy pony. The biggest of them could have fit a draft horse inside his belly.

They ringed around the half-angels and golden eyes pinned Marion.

"Maybe I should stay," Nori whispered.

"That won't be necessary." Marion squeezed her cousin's hand. "You'll get in touch if Violet has questions about the wedding?" They'd made a new statuette that allowed them to communicate from different planes. Using the equivalent of a magical telephone was more convenient than summoning Nori every time Marion needed to say something.

"Yeah, I can call you," Nori said. "If you really want me to go."

"I do." Marion would have an easier time sneaking around the sanctuary if she was alone.

Nori vanished into the ley lines, and Marion followed her escorts into the valley. The sanctuary was so small that there were no cars, and most shifters could travel faster on steep terrain on four legs anyway. But that left Marion trudging down steep trails into the cleft between mountains on foot. She thanked the gods—Seth in particular, with some amusement—that she'd thought to wear pants rather than one of her lovely-but-ridiculous dresses. She'd never have been able to make it down the slope on heels.

The path weaved in and out of trees, concealing the village for minutes at a time. The roar of the waterfall never left them completely, but it quieted by the time they'd walked for almost an hour. They emerged in a grassy field filled with frolicking shifter children.

A few of the bigger pups stopped to stare when Marion passed. She wondered how many of them she should have known.

Then the Academy appeared at the end of the road.

It was the tallest structure in the village, and the only one protected by tall fencing topped by spikes. The rest of the village was a socialist's dream of communal living. Only the school where they housed the preternatural community's treasured youth lived under higher security.

The gates were closed when Marion and the shifters finally stopped outside of them. Two names were picked out atop the arch in iron scrollwork: Gresham and Wilder. The sight of the second name made Marion's stomach flip.

Someone must have been watching the security cameras because the gate swung open as soon as Marion approached. Nothing but lawn separated her from the gabled roofs and sprawling brick-walled wings of the Academy, and she waited for familiarity to set in.

Nothing struck except a faint sense of dread.

A man that Marion didn't know was waiting on the front steps. He had skin the color of a latte and hard eyes—eyes that were not shifter gold, she was surprised to see. As soon as she hit the bottom of the steps with the wolves at her side, he spun and marched into the Academy silently.

She followed. The wolves didn't.

"I'm here to see Rylie," she said.

"I know." His voice was so deep that it ached painfully within her chest.

This strange man took Marion to a room left of the entrance. He pushed her inside and shut the door.

Marion found herself in a tearoom with eleven people: ten shifters in their human forms ringing the walls, and a lone middle-aged woman on a sofa at the center of the office.

Rylie Gresham.

"Please, sit," Rylie said.

There was tea on the table between them.

Guards ringing the room.

This wasn't a social visit.

Marion sat slowly, even though she felt very strange being so stiff, so formal. She had described Rylie in her journals as "like my mom, except not as horrible as Ariane." Marion had written that when she was eleven. *Eleven.* Teenage rebellion against her birth mother had struck early.

Not against Rylie, though. Marion and Dana had grown up alongside Rylie's multitude of children. They'd spent every summer at the werewolf sanctuary. Marion had even attended the Academy for a year, though she'd done it more as a way to indulge Rylie's wish that Marion would have formal education, not because she'd felt she needed it.

Now Rylie was treating her like a political guest, bringing out the good china and having their visit supervised. They were even holding the meeting at the Academy itself, which had the only formal meeting rooms in the entire sanctuary.

"How can I help you?" Rylie looked maternal, if not quite unassuming, in her nude-colored skirt suit. Her voice was pitched low, her hair brushed out straight, her vibrant golden eyes intent.

"It's about Deirdre Tombs's preternatural cooperative," Marion said.

"I thought it would be. Tea?"

"No, thank you."

Rylie poured a cup for herself and sat back. "You must be wondering why I agreed to Deirdre's council. Right?"

The reasoning behind Rylie's support of the council was unimportant. It was too late to undo any of that. "Actually, I've come to explain why you must vote for Konig to remain Prince of the Autumn Court."

"I'm listening," Rylie said.

"I've done what I can to protect the Winter Court refugees, but my control over the plane's magic is limited. I was unable to stop Leliel from invading Niflheimr. Many refugees were lost."

"I heard about that." Rylie's voice had gone softer. "I'm sorry, Marion."

"Once Konig and I marry, he'll be able to take over the wards," Marion said. "He'll be able to reinforce them and allow the unseelie to flourish in the Winter Court again. Also, the Ethereal Levant has a peace treaty with the Autumn Court. If we can extend the peace treaty to the Winter Court, then we can ensure that she doesn't hurt us again."

"I understand that extension of the peace treaty is the only reason why you're planning to marry Prince ErlKonig."

Marion was prepared for that accusation, gentle as Rylie made it sound. "I won't deny it's a factor, but Konig and I plan to marry because we love one another." Never mind the fact she would have dumped him on his ass if Leliel hadn't attacked. She was glad for the outcome, in a morbid sort of way. Things had never been better with Konig.

"I'm happy for you." It sounded genuine. Maybe. It was hard to tell. "I got your invitation, by the way. Thank you. I'm thrilled to attend."

"That's assuming the vote doesn't ruin our plans. Did Deirdre frighten you with the idea of a second god-scale disaster?"

"She tried," Rylie said, "but I knew Elise and James as well as anyone. Elise is a true hero. She would never hurt anyone unnecessarily. In her hands, we're safe."

"Then why the vote?"

"I know Deirdre very well, too." Rylie took a long drink of her tea, but it wasn't enough to mask the lines of tension between her eyebrows and bracketing the sides of her mouth. She was upset about something.

Marion wondered if Deirdre had blackmail material on Rylie. What could the werewolf Alpha have done that would be worthy of such a drastic vote?

It was hard to remember that Rylie wasn't as pure as she looked. This was the woman who'd cheated on Seth and fallen pregnant with his brother's get. She'd left him at the altar. And he was still broken over it years later.

Rylie was better than Marion at pretending to be innocent, but Marion knew the truth.

"Help me protect the refugees. Endorse Konig and publicly bless our wedding." Marion hadn't meant to be as blunt about the request, but now that the moment had arrived, she didn't know how else to ask it.

"Are you sure you don't want tea?" Rylie asked.

"Very well," she said, trying to keep the irritation out of her voice and off of her face.

Rylie poured. Her graceful movements were most likely calculated, part of the same maternal image she cultivated in her dress and speech. As she took care of the tea, she said, "I can't make a public endorsement. It isn't shifter business. I've already planned to vote in your favor, though."

"You have?"

"I told you that I know Elise well," Rylie said.

"The woman I remember wouldn't cause another god-level tragedy over your wedding. She'd want you to be happy, Marion. She'd support your marriage to Konig if that was what it took to keep you happy."

"I hope you're right," Marion murmured into her cup of tea. The sip she took was especially bitter.

A hand touched her knee. The last time someone had done that to her, it had been Seth, trying to comfort her after his inability to diagnose her memory loss. But this was Rylie. Their contact made the guards nervous. For the first time, they moved against the walls, rocking on their feet, reaching for weapons.

There was nothing but kindness in Rylie's eyes. "It's okay to be afraid. All the sane people are afraid to marry under normal circumstances. You'll have the eyes of the world on you during and after."

She clenched her teacup in both hands. "I'm not afraid."

"Marion..." Rylie shifted onto the couch next to her. She wrapped an arm around her shoulders. "You're going to be okay."

Unexpected tears plucked at Marion's eyes.

Maybe this was why Marion had written that Rylie was like her mother, but better. Because this was exactly the kind of conversation Marion would have wanted to have with Ariane, if Ariane would have reached out to her. But Ariane was conspicuously absent and nobody knew how to reach her.

"How do I know if marriage is the right thing to do?" Marion asked.

"You don't. Nobody does." With one more squeeze, Rylie let her go. She stood and became formal again. Rylie glanced at the clock on the wall, positioned between the shoulders of two of her silent guards. "I regret to run so soon, but I have plans."

"Can I stay for a little while?" Marion asked. "I've been trying to spend some time in places I used to know well to see if they'll jog my memories."

It was such a bold lie that Rylie must have been capable of scenting it, but the werewolf Alpha didn't look at all suspicious. "I understand completely. Please feel free to explore. My people will be happy to get you back to the ley line juncture whenever you're ready—no rush."

After Rylie left, Marion wasted time by wandering through the Sanctuary Academy. The gardens were tended by young witches and were almost as lush as anything in the sidhe courts. Many students were already studying outside, lolling in the warmth, wolf among human, panther and deer curled together.

There was a quality to the air that exhilarated Marion—something that was not quite smell, nor was it the musical hum of magic from the Middle Worlds.

She circled the halls, trying to figure out what she sensed that so excited her. Marion's fingertips tingled with it.

A voice caught her attention, and she stopped in front of a door, peering through its window. The students were seated in a circle of power. One of them was in the middle, caught mid-shapeshift, while the instructor lectured on what was happening.

The light of rapt attention glowed around the students.

Learning.

That was what so enticed Marion. It was the heady buzz of knowledge blooming. Being exposed to it made Marion feel more refreshed than if she had slept twelve hours and woken to espresso and an hour of yoga.

If she hadn't had an agenda, she could have lingered to watch the students learning to shapeshift for days without end.

Marion must have required little coercion to spend a year studying at the Academy. Between Rylie, the mother-who-was-not-her-mother that actually gave Marion the attention she craved, and an environment fertile for learning, it would have been relative paradise. Far from the lonely libraries Marion kept at her home on Vancouver Island, the Academy was vibrant and alive.

She must have loved being there.

Nothing looked familiar during Marion's laps,

but she hadn't expected anything to. There were no memories to jog within Marion's skull. They hadn't been lost in some shadowy corner of her brain like books improperly catalogued in a library. They had been extracted and stuck into the Canope.

Now the Canope was broken. Those memories were gone. The best she could hope to accomplish was studying her journals the way a medical student studied anatomy and pretending that she knew what she was doing.

There were other things to get from the Academy, though.

Marion had found diagrams of its layout before her visit, and those guided her through the halls. She had a very specific destination: the administrative offices on the first floor, opposite the gender-segregated student dormitories.

Marion didn't look at anyone as she glided through the halls. She kept her back straight, chin lifted. Many students looked at her, though. They lived there during the school year—the period of time that fell between August and May—and they knew when people were neither staff nor student.

Someone would also know what her eyes meant, so whispers about her presence would spread quickly.

She needed to be out of the administrative offices before that happened.

Her visit with Rylie Gresham had been timed for eleven in the morning, and the administrative offices shut down at noon for lunch. Marion had allowed enough time to pass while exploring. She reached the office when a man wearing business casual was hanging an "out to lunch" sign on the outer office doors.

"Can I help you?" He smiled at Marion.

She smiled back at him and let the full force of her energy shine. "No thank you."

He looked dazed, but managed to walk away without falling over.

Marion took his place in front of the door and knocked on it. Nothing happened. "*Merde*," she muttered.

Her ability to open doors by knocking was god-given, and that meant that if the gods weren't paying attention, it had zero impact. Elise didn't care if Marion got into the admin offices.

Marion reached into the energy that flowed through the Academy as one of its witch students might, tapping into it as she focused on a rune.

"Open," she said as she grabbed the knob.

The lock opened with a flare of magic that any witch in the Academy would feel if they were paying attention.

Marion was in.

She didn't waste time with the computers in the front offices. She went straight to the principal's room in the back, whose name ("Summer Gresham") suggested more than a hint of nepotism at work at the Academy.

Who was this Summer woman? One of Rylie's actual daughters? Someone who had grown up adored by a powerful, maternal Alpha werewolf?

Marion was shocked by how jealous it made her feel to know there were people who had grown up in the privilege of Rylie's care. People who were not Marion, rejected by a mother who wouldn't even attend her wedding.

At least Rylie would be there.

Marion grabbed the doorknob. "Open," she said again.

And it did.

Summer Gresham's office made it look as though she was working from the inside of a giant computer. Every wall was covered in metal cages filled with a tangle of cables, blinking lights, and buzzing fans. Her floor was twelve inches above the floor in the hallway outside. The temperature was warmer and dryer than outside, too. Her desk was little more than a chair in front of a table big enough to hold an energy drink.

Strange as it looked, the office glowed with as much knowledge as the more rustic classrooms outside. Regardless of her title, Summer Gresham was a woman in the business of acquiring information. The lifeblood of angels.

Marion's nose wrinkled as she swept the trash off of Summer's desk. She used a tissue to wipe down the keyboard. Then she sat gingerly and rolled up to the monitor.

Summer had left herself logged in.

"Such trust," Marion murmured. But why shouldn't she trust? She was in the heart of the blissful shapeshifter sanctuary, an area secured against all enemies.

There was an icon for the OPA database on the desktop. Marion clicked.

The interface wasn't entirely unfamiliar. Marion had been required to fill out a few forms on computers at the United Nations during the summit, and it seemed to use the same sort of program. She easily found the database search.

"Goat...woman..." Marion said to herself as she typed. She felt a bit stupid about it.

She felt slightly less stupid when the search brought up several results.

Five individual demons, one entire class of demons, and three shifters.

"Oh my."

Marion took out her cell phone and plugged it into the computer. She didn't need to be a hacker to copy the records over within minutes.

That should have been all that Marion risked. Sanctuary witches may have already alerted Rylie to what she was up to. It was time to run home to study the files on goat-looking women. But she had access to so much information, and she was still giddy from the brush of energy she'd felt in the school.

Marion typed her own name into the OPA search field.

There was one primary record, which she copied over to her phone's memory. That one file took much longer than the nine listings for "goat women."

While it downloaded, she skimmed the notes.

There were a staggering number of personal

testimonies submitted by OPA allies talking about Marion. The testimony at the top had been submitted by Rylie. It was a video, which played as soon as Marion clicked on it.

Rylie had been filmed somewhere that looked like a living room. "Now?" she asked the camera, patting her straight blond hair to neaten it. "Right now?"

A voice off-screen said, "Whenever you're ready."

"Yes, she's dangerous," Rylie said, as though answering a question that had been asked before filming. "I've watched her grow up, and she's had sleepovers with my kids, but—what do you expect me to say, Fritz?"

"I want to know if you think we can trust her," said the man, presumably Fritz. "What threat level is she?"

"The highest," Rylie said. "You should absolutely be prepared to kill her. I have been for years. We'd be stupid if we weren't prepared to kill Marion Garin."

SEVEN

Most people stopped when they hit Rock Bottom. Seth went lower. He wrapped his wounds in cotton and leather and descended to the recesses of his past.

With a snap of his fingers, he returned to the werewolf sanctuary.

Seth remembered the last time that he had visited the sanctuary outside Northgate. He'd left Las Vegas while UNLV had been on winter break, hoping to get insight into a case he was working with the police. It hadn't been the case that had broken him—the one with the vampires, with all the blood—but it had been the one right before that. And he had been considering moving back to the sanctuary.

He'd arrived from dry, barren Nevada to find Northgate buried under snow taller than he was.

Everyone at the sanctuary had been assigned to shoveling duty. Even after Genesis, when Rylie had snowplows at her disposal, the pack had still preferred manual labor.

Seth had grabbed a shovel and jumped in out of habit. That was just life at the sanctuary. Everyone worked together to make things happen. They were one big family, even if it had become far bigger after Genesis.

Rylie had been working one of the smaller side roads. The Alpha still hadn't been too good to do her own work, and she'd been happy to have Seth join in.

"Our security's been great," Rylie had said to him. "The wards do a lot of the work. Then we rotate out nightly schedules with patrols, just like we used to with the cooking." Her hair had been trapped under a saggy knitted hat, but a few flyaway strands had floated around cheeks pinkened by cold.

Even wrapped in multitude of layers of winter gear, her form had been petite but strong, both fragile and unbreakable.

Her belly must have been swelling with her next child, but Seth hadn't been able to tell that under the jacket.

"Are you even listening to me?" Rylie had asked, not unkindly.

He hadn't been. He'd just been looking at her, drinking in the sight of the woman who had once been his world. "Sorry. What did you say?"

She'd reached up to pull his hat over his ears,

then swipe her gloved hands over his shoulders to clear snow away. "I said security is fine. Everything is fine. Thank you for checking. That's not the only reason you came back, is it?"

Not the only reason, but the most important.

Seth had been imagining that things couldn't be going well at the sanctuary after Genesis. Rylie had been put in the position of handling thousands upon thousands of new preternaturals —mostly shifters—and the volume should have been overwhelming.

He'd spent all semester at UNLV imagining the struggle at the sanctuary. Having Abel for support couldn't have been much support at all. Abel had always been bad at logistics, and thinking, and anything else that didn't involve shooting things.

Seth had expected Rylie to ask for help.

She hadn't.

Rylie had said, "Everything is fine." And she'd kept shoveling, accompanied by hundreds of shifters.

That had been more than a decade ago. He hadn't gone to the sanctuary since, nor had he spoken to Rylie. But he returned to the sanctuary after his talk with Lucifer at Rock Bottom.

Seth arrived on the road from Northgate, right where it broke through the pass. He was surprised that he could get there. Nobody should have been able to teleport inside the wards—even Seth. But he couldn't even feel them pushing back. One of the benefits of being a god, he supposed.

So he appeared on the road in a swirl of brimstone smoke, about two miles closer to the sanctuary than he'd expected, and the sight of his past basically punched him in the face.

Everything was old, but new.

The same mountains, the same waterfall, the same fields. Same old cottages that he'd helped build by hand.

But there were new cottages too, and even an apartment building. He saw a white square of a building that must have been a hospital—something they'd never had in his time there, since it wasn't like the average shifter needed much medical care. Even though he couldn't see the school from there, a sign directing him up the road toward the Academy meant it existed. That had always been Rylie's dream. A school. A way to teach the shifter kids. A place for them to belong.

She had everything she'd always wanted.

Ten years later, Rylie still didn't need Seth.

He saw nothing but unfamiliar faces on his way into town. New people were weirder than new buildings. Seth had always known the entire pack.

He hadn't called ahead, so Rylie wasn't expecting him and he didn't have a meeting place established. But he knew where she was. He could feel her presence in the way that he could feel all of the other lives around him—the long threads unspooling as time marched onward. All were vibrant in the way that only gaean lives could be.

None were as vibrant as that of the Alpha.

He followed the gleaming thread of her life toward the waterfall.

By the time he ended up walking among the cottages, things looked so unchanged that Seth could almost convince himself that it was the old days again. He'd built many of those roofs and hung most of the doors. The cottages were uniform in Rylie's taste: gold with white trim and protective pentacles over the windows.

The road sloped down, drawing him nearer the beach.

New cottages had been built in the style of the old ones, pushing the neighborhood nearer to the lake. But the lake itself was still pristine, untouched. It stretched toward the cliff face from which the waterfall sprang.

One end of the beach was busy with children playing under the watchful eye of the babysitter. The rockier end was uninhabited.

Except for *her*.

Seth stood on the edge of the rocks for a long time—gods only knew how long. He wasn't paying attention to the passage of heartbeats and fading of lives.

He let himself drink in the sight of the werewolf Alpha sitting on a rocky outcropping, leaning forward on her hands. A suit jacket was puddled on the rocks beside her. She'd kicked her shoes off and left them soles-up on top of the jacket. Her hair hung in a glossy sheet over her shoulders, long and straight.

Without being able to see her face, Rylie

almost looked like the girl he'd met at summer camp back when she'd been just fifteen years old. Right after she had been bitten by a werewolf.

She straightened slowly, as if aware she was being watched. Her head tipped back.

Rylie was smelling the air.

He heard the quick intake of her breath. He saw the way she went still, as if afraid to move and break the moment.

Then she twisted. The face peering at him from the rocks was a little rounder, a little more lined, but still *hers*.

"Seth," Rylie whispered.

"Does it hurt?" Rylie asked. It was the first thing she'd managed to say in five minutes.

Seth let the hem of his shirt drop, concealing the wound left by the Hounds. "Yeah."

"Oh, Seth," she said, still barely above a whisper. It was strange to hear the Alpha talking like she couldn't breathe.

She hadn't seen him in ten years, aside from the moment at the summit, but he'd seen her in glimpses. Always on the news or on the back jacket of her autobiography. Every time, she'd been in leader mode, her most glorious persona. After the years she'd spent struggling to take ownership of her power as Alpha, it was incredible to see that come to fruition.

Now she was a teenage girl again, uncertain in the face of painful changes.

This girl was no "girl" anymore. She was in her forties and looked every inch of it. She was also every inch as beautiful as the lake that they sat beside, right next to each other, the way that they used to as kids.

Gorgeous.

Except for the fact she looked so horrified.

"That's why I need your help," Seth said.

"What did Genesis do to you?" Her forefinger traced the corner of his eyes, the space between his eyebrows, the edge of his lips. The exact places where Rylie's skin was getting its deepest furrows.

"It wasn't Genesis. It was Elise," Seth said.

She lifted a shoulder in a half-shrug. "Six of one..."

"I'm like her," Seth said, lowering his voice. He knew that the shifter kids playing on the beach were too far away to hear—shifter senses didn't develop fully until puberty—but he couldn't help it. "I'm like both of them. The third."

Rylie's lips parted. She exhaled slowly. "*Oh.* Another triad."

There had been three gods before Genesis too. Adam, Eve, and Lilith had represented the three major factions: gaeans, angels, and demons respectively. The three of them had never gotten along. Those personality clashes had been what ultimately led to Elise killing them, and Genesis in general.

"It seems like the universe needs a triad," Seth

said. "Guess which one I am."

"You're like Lilith, round two." Rylie leaned her head against his shoulder. And she said again, "Oh, Seth."

The sympathy felt better than he would have expected. "Not exactly like Lilith. I seem to be mortal for the moment."

"You came to Earth as an avatar."

"Is that what it's called?" Another thought struck him. "How would you know that?"

"I've been in contact with Elise and James since Genesis. We've talked about a few things."

"Through Marion?" Seth asked.

Rylie's eyebrows crimped. "Yes, through Marion." What little composure the Alpha had began to crumble. "Why would you have come back to talk to her? Why not me, or your brother, or Abram, or...*anyone*? We thought you were dead!"

"She found me first. I wouldn't have talked to anyone if I could have avoided it."

"Marion told me what you've been doing in Ransom Falls." Rylie bit her bottom lip hard enough that the teeth left dents. "You could have told me. I wouldn't have bothered you."

"I had reasons to hide." He patted his chest. "Speaking of which, I'm still hiding. Don't tell anyone I'm around."

"I never speak to Elise directly, so you don't need to worry about that."

"She's not the only one I'm hiding from now." Dana McIntyre was a child who'd grown up fostered in the sanctuary environment too, after all.

"I hope you'll tell me everything that you're dealing with soon." Rylie's fingers inched over the coarse rock toward his. "I understand why you might not want to yet. And every resource I have at my disposal belongs to you. If there's anything I can do to help, Seth, you only have to ask me." Her eyes were the same color as the summer sunlight. "*Anything.*"

"You can start by having witches heal my human body." They wouldn't be able to save him completely—nobody could—but they would give him more time to decide if he wanted to take Lucifer up on his offer.

"Done," Rylie said.

Their fingers overlapped on the rock, just a little.

Rylie had to dismiss a dozen guards before she could take Seth anywhere in private. Even then, privacy with the Alpha werewolf at her sanctuary was not much privacy at all; all those unfamiliar faces that had ignored Seth on his way into town were interested now that he was with Rylie. Even taking the back roads, they passed dozens of shifters on their way to the Academy.

"The whole valley is structured to encourage socializing," Rylie said apologetically. "We've found that shifters live longer, happier, healthier lives if we're forced to be close together."

"It's only been fifteen years. You haven't had a lot of time for experimentation."

"We ended up with a shocking number of senior citizens returning from Genesis as preternaturals. We've dealt with more end-of-life care for shifters than you'd expect."

Seth actually did expect that. He'd seen his fair share of it in Ransom Falls. "Is that why you have a hospital?"

Rylie nodded. "We're employing Whytes again. Can you believe it?"

"Whytes? People related to Scott and Stephanie? *Really*?"

"Really. We've got Stephanie's cousins from the Half Moon Bay Coven."

Scott Whyte had been a therapist—and a witch—who had treated Rylie early in her werewolf life. Stephanie was his daughter, an emergency room doctor who had partially inspired Seth to pursue medicine. Both had ultimately betrayed the pack. Betrayal had been a common theme before Genesis, though. War between gods had radiated through the entire world, from the most important people to the most trivial, and it had hurt everyone.

"How can you be sure they're trustworthy?" Seth asked.

"They've changed since Genesis. Everything has changed." She bit her bottom lip and turned her gaze to her feet as they headed up the dirt road.

Even with the reminder that Seth was one of those things that had changed, it was nice to talk old stuff with Rylie like that. People they used to know. And they were doing it in a place where they used to share a life together.

A place where Rylie didn't need him.

"I have a class of witches at the Academy too," Rylie said. "Graduates teach underclassmen. That's why we're heading there. Our coven is excellent and will be able to heal you if anyone can." Her eyes flicked up to him. "Abel isn't home, but he'll be back soon if you want to see him. I know he'd like to see you."

If Rylie really thought that Abel would want to see him, she was being optimistic.

Seth wasn't sure he'd want to see Abel, either.

"I'll think on it," he said.

Rylie rewarded him with a smile like sunshine breaking through clouds.

They reached the fence protecting the Academy. Seth took a moment to admire it while Rylie keyed in a code to open the gate. When they'd talked schools back in the day, he'd imagined something like a one-room schoolhouse. This was not a one-room anything. More like a hundred-room facility. A thousand rooms. It sprawled through the forest as far as he could see, and the gardens at its rear extended beyond that. The warded fence protected another small lake, and enough fields for all of the school's shifters to run free on the moons.

"We have over fourteen hundred students in residence. We're building another wing so we can accommodate more." Rylie stepped back as the gate swung open. "You can see Golden Lake over there."

The summer camps where Rylie and Seth met had been called Golden Lake and Silver Brook. "Isn't that an ominous name?"

"It's acknowledging history," Rylie said. "I had to keep a piece of that around when everything else was gone. Come on, the witches are in the south wing."

Even though the Academy was younger than Genesis, and hardly an antique, it had been designed to look almost like an old ski lodge. It was open, warm, comfortable. Lots of low chairs and big windows. Seth took a deep breath when they entered the atrium, and the musky scent of werewolves almost overwhelmed him with nostalgia.

He also smelled something like burning oak and lavender. That smell didn't belong with the others.

"Most kids are outside for lunch right now," Rylie explained as she waved and smiled at students. They were scattered around the atrium, reading on tablet devices, lying underneath potted trees, playing hacky-sack. None of them looked particularly awed to see the Alpha in their midst. Apparently she wasn't an unusual visitor.

The smell of burning oak only grew stronger as they headed toward the south wing.

"Is Nash home?" Seth asked. Nashriel was Rylie's son-in-law, an angel who had married her oldest daughter.

"He hasn't been for a while," Rylie said. "Why do you ask?"

Smoky, woody smells almost always meant angels. If Seth could detect it with his non-werewolf nose, then it must have been recent. "No reason," he started to say.

Then they passed the administrative offices and the door opened. Seth and Rylie almost tripped over the woman who emerged.

She must not have expected to see anyone in the hallway. She looked guilty. "Hello again, Rylie." And then her eyes moved to him, and her jaw dropped. "Seth."

"Marion," he said. "Hi."

EIGHT

Marion's time recovering in bed from anemia had been long and tedious. Boredom was a challenging thing for a half-angel. She'd occupied herself with books on witchcraft and one timeless day with Konig, but it was poor replacement for the kind of adventuresome lifestyle to which she was accustomed.

Worse than bored, she'd been lonely.

Seth had vanished after the incident in Sheol and hadn't visited while she was healing. Not once.

Now here he was, walking around the werewolf sanctuary with the Alpha herself—the woman who pretended to be like Marion's mother, even while telling the OPA that they needed ways to kill her.

Even so, Marion forgot to hold a grudge. She

was too relieved to see Seth whole and alive and passably mortal.

"Thank the gods!" She flung her arms around his neck in a tight embrace. He staggered as if surprised. It took him a moment to pat her on the back, but his weak laugh was almost as relieved as how she felt.

He still smelled like leather and gunpowder.

"Gentle," Seth warned, though he squeezed her tightly. "I'm not back to normal yet. Whatever normal is."

She stepped back but didn't release him. If Marion had her way, she'd be hanging on to his arms until he swore up and down to never go missing ever again. "Are you okay?"

"I'm fine for now." He patted his chest. "I'm not healing, though."

Marion didn't need to see under the shirt to know that he was touching wounds inflicted by the same Hounds that had nearly killed her. They would have eaten him if she hadn't intervened.

"What were you doing in there?" Rylie's voice was an unpleasant reminder that she still existed.

Marion looped her arm through Seth's and held him firmly, staring right into Rylie's eyes. Among werewolves, that kind of eye contact was considered a play for dominance. "It's unimportant. I was just on my way out. How lucky to have encountered you two, though. I didn't expect to see you here, Seth."

"Rylie's witches are going to help fix me up," Seth said. "Make sure that I don't die."

"*Her* witches? Why didn't you come to me?"

He carefully disengaged his arm from hers. "I was pretty sure you wouldn't want to see me. Because, you know..." He pointed at his teeth, and her neck, making the kind of expression that belonged on a Halloween vampire mask.

"That's patently ridiculous. You should realize by now that I'd always want to see you."

Seth jammed his hands into his pockets. "You can't blame me for thinking that might have changed, all things considered."

"I can and do blame you," Marion said.

"We have places to be," Rylie interrupted. "The witches won't be around all day, Seth."

Marion forced a smile. "Then let's go see them."

"You're not invited," Rylie said.

"I'm not asking for an invitation. I don't know how you've vetted your witches, so they won't work on my friend unless I review their techniques."

"*Your* friend?" Rylie glanced between Seth and Marion, her eyebrows climbing her forehead.

"I'd appreciate having Marion's opinion," Seth said.

Rylie could have shut Seth down. God on Earth or not, Seth wasn't Alpha. It wasn't his sanctuary, his Academy, his home, or his witches. But she said, "If that's what you want, Seth," and there was a strange pitch to Rylie's voice.

She didn't *need* to defer to Seth, but she was going to.

If Marion had been a werewolf, that would have been the moment her hackles lifted.

Instead, she took Seth's arm again, and he didn't pull away from her.

"Excellent," Marion said coolly. "Let's see what sort of so-called witches the sanctuary employs."

Between the Winter Court and her home on Vancouver Island, Marion wasn't lacking for ritual space, but she still lusted over the Academy's altar.

It resided in a room big enough to hold all of the North American Union's covens at once, with one wall open to the forest, a cliff, and the private lake. All of the elements were represented nearby: fire held captive in basins, earth below, sky above, water in the lake. Even the stone of the mountains and the iron curls embedded in the floor would offer different kinds of energy to feed all rituals. At night, the moon would shine through the dome of glass that the sun currently beamed from. Golden motes drifted through the air.

But the altar. The *altar*.

It was a multi-leveled thing of marble beauty. Its glass bowls cradled crystals aging through phases of the moon. The cloths were spun with silver thread that shimmered like water.

Marion was awed until the witch standing on the altar turned.

"Sinead McGrath," Marion snarled. She

recognized her from the sparse descriptions in her old journals—specifically, in the pink vitiligo patterning her otherwise tanned skin. A shock of white hair flowed over her right ear.

The witch's eyes narrowed. "Marion Garin."

Sinead was a stronger witch than Marion would have expected to find in Rylie's employ—strong enough that she had felt she could rival Marion's power. And she very nearly could.

But only nearly.

"You're going to let *her* work on Seth?" Marion asked.

"Work on whom?" Sinead asked.

"My friend," Rylie said. "Abel's brother. He was made into a golem during Genesis, and he needs to be repaired."

Marion opened her mouth to argue, but Seth nudged her. He shook his head once he had her attention.

"I've never seen a golem so detailed before," Sinead said. "I'm not sure I'll be able to help."

"Wait here a moment," Rylie said to Seth. "I need to hash out details with my high priestess." The Alpha took Sinead behind the altar so they could discuss what work Seth needed performed without Marion's intrusion. The motive was so transparent that Marion was tempted to butt in just to prove that she could.

"Golem?" Marion whispered.

"I don't want anyone but Rylie to know who I am," Seth whispered back. "So yeah. Golem." His gaze flicked to Marion's throat more than once. He must have been looking for scarring from when he had drunk her blood. "Who's Sinead McGrath to you? Is this witch a problem?"

"Only because she's a jerk," Marion said. "She bleached several of my finest dresses when I attended the Academy. And then she had the nerve to lobby for student body high priestess. The slanderous campaign she ran..."

"How do you even know about that?"

"I wrote more in my journals about Sinead than I wrote about the times I saved Rylie from assassination."

"Of course you did," Seth said. Marion was certain that she wasn't imagining how fond he sounded. "Sinead McGrath is a good witch, though?"

"Probably." Marion wouldn't have wasted time feuding with someone who wasn't excellent at magic, especially since she could have hexed anyone else off the face of the planet for screwing with her wardrobe.

"Who won as student body high priestess?" Seth asked.

"I'm surprised you'd even have to ask. I did. I always win."

"Not always," he said soberly.

She traced her hands along the unbroken skin on her throat. "We survived. That's a win."

"But the Canope. Your memories. You shouldn't have done that for me."

"There was no other choice," Marion said.

"I don't think I can die. Not permanently,

anyway. I'd just lose my body and..." He pointed to the sky and an imaginary Heaven where gods might have resided.

"Neither of us knew that at the time. We still don't know that."

Seth shrugged it off, like there was no point trying to argue something he believed to be fact. "When I was carrying the Canope, I picked up on some of your memories. Elise wanted you to find me. You wouldn't do it. She emptied your mind and left nothing but my name so you'd find me."

Unpleasant cold washed over Marion's shoulders. "No, it couldn't have been her." She'd just gotten used to the idea that Elise wasn't out to get her. Being told she was wrong—that a god did want to hurt her—made her stomach lurch. "I found one of the assassins—Geoff Samuelson. He said that some goat-woman confronted me."

"A goat?"

"A goat-woman. Yes." She lowered her voice. "That's why I was in the office. I was using the OPA databases to download creature files onto my phone. If I can find her, maybe I can get answers."

"It's not what your memories showed me," Seth said. "Elise was so angry that she struck you."

Marion touched her cheek reflexively. It was like her body remembered the blow even if her mind didn't. "But I wouldn't do what she told me."

"You didn't even know me, but you stuck up for me. And the way I thanked you for it..." His gaze dropped to her throat again.

Marion's memory of her time in the Dead

Forest of Sheol was hazy. It was little more than a sensation of walking through a long corridor toward a doorway.

Seth had stood between her and that door. He hadn't let her die.

"Do you still want to hurt me?" Marion asked.

"Not at all. I don't understand why I did when I was in Sheol."

"You're clearly some kind of death god, and I was dying. You were operating on instincts that told you to finish the job. I don't blame you." After a moment's hesitation, she took his hands. "You didn't need to run from me. I wish you would let me help."

"I might need your help yet," Seth said. "If I wanted root access to the darknet, could you hook me up?"

Yet another mention of the darknet. It couldn't be coincidence. "No way."

"Yeah, I get it." He looked abashed.

"No, it's not about you. It's because I don't know where the servers are, but you're not the first person this week to look for them. I've searched Niflheimr top to bottom for them, and even searched the bedroom of the former administrators, but I've got no clue. Pierce and Jaycee Hardwick left no clues behind." Marion laughed shakily. "It seems like everybody wants the darknet at this point. The American Gaean Commission is searching, and Jibril thinks Leliel wants access as well."

"Lucifer's the one who asked me for it," Seth

said. "He's the leader of the vampires."

Marion knew who Lucifer was. She'd been seated next to him at the summit. "Why would he ask you, of all people?"

"Because I asked a favor of him first," Seth said.

Rylie and Sinead returned before he could elaborate.

"The coven is on the way," Rylie said. "Sinead is pretty certain they can slow the decay. They've got a healer in the group and Sinead's good with constructs. Between the two of them, they should be able to fix your avatar."

"Words like 'pretty certain' and 'should' don't comfort me very much," Marion said.

Sinead's hatred was painted all over her face, but her tone was carefully civilized. "We've been studying the craft at the Academy for years and have broken new ground on gaean magic. If you think you have anything to contribute, though, don't be afraid to jump in."

It was a challenge.

A few months earlier, that was a challenge Marion would have happily risen to meet.

Unfortunately, since she was studying everything secondhand from the internet, Marion knew less magic than an adept at the Academy, and far less than Sinead.

It was arrogance that had driven Sinead and Marion to rivalry while at school. Marion couldn't fix what she'd done in the past—just like Sinead couldn't bring back Marion's dresses—but she could swallow her pride and take the chance to learn a little more magic from someone with greater mastery of it than her.

"I'll just watch from the sidelines, if that's okay," Marion said.

Surprise lifted Sinead's eyebrows. There was a slash of white through one that corresponded with the pattern of her vitiligo. "Yeah. I think that'll be okay."

Seth squeezed Marion's hand encouragingly.

"Then let's do this," he said.

It took twenty minutes for the coven to arrive from around the school. It was more than the traditional number of twelve—more like twenty, Seth determined after a quick count. Not all of them took position within the circle of power so the extras must have been students.

"Are you comfortable using this as a teaching opportunity?" Rylie asked. She was sitting in the center of the altar with Seth.

"Working on a 'golem' is a hell of a lesson, don't you think?"

Rylie smiled faintly. "It wouldn't be the strangest lesson we've had at the Academy." She sounded proud, as well she should have. A school of witches, werewolves, and angels—that was likely to be her legacy, even after her legislative impact had faded into the past.

"You can include anyone you like," Seth said. "I trust you."

"And Marion too," Rylie said.

The half-angel was talking to Sinead in the back corner of the room. It obviously wasn't a comfortable conversation. They stood a good eight feet apart with such guarded body language that they might as well have both been wearing armor. But they *were* talking.

"I trust her, yeah. She's a good person," Seth said.

"She's not good or bad. She's a person."

"What's that supposed to mean?"

"I've had Marion in my home every summer since she was five years old. I know her too well to say she's good or trustworthy."

"Harsh."

"I'm a parent," Rylie said. "I've learned that sometimes the kindest thing you can do for a child is to be harsh on them."

There was nothing childish in the way that Marion spoke to Sinead with impassioned fervor. She was gesturing with her hands now, illustrating concepts by etching symbols in the air with her fingertips, which occasionally sparked with glimmering magic.

She looked graver than she had when Seth had met her in his hospital, with all her wide-eyed confusion. Things had happened to her. She'd walked *this* close to death. And soon, she'd be married to an unseelie prince. Marion was young, but far from a kid.

"Then let's try it that way," Sinead said loudly enough that everyone in the room could hear it. "Let's get in the circle."

The witches gathered. Rylie and Seth got to their feet. "I should get out of the way," Rylie said. "You're in good hands." She brushed his shoulder when she stepped down from the altar.

The sensations he'd been trying to ignore roared to the forefront of his mind—the cable of life that wound through Rylie and connected her to the surrounding world.

There was death in Rylie's past.

Before Genesis, Rylie had fought beside Elise on the edge of the world. They had conflicted with angels—Leliel among their number—and one of them had stabbed Rylie. She'd been saved by the gods, similar to the way that Seth had been saved. Rylie had kept her mortality, though. Unlike a vampire, she was alive, not undead. That meant death loomed in her future as well as her past. Her tenure as Alpha was bookended by oblivion.

If he wanted, he could know how Rylie was going to die. Again. Permanently, this time.

Seth shoved the sensations away, trying to focus on the here and now. On Marion's heart-shaped face looming over the heads of the other witches. She looked worried, but when she realized he was watching, she offered a dimpled smile.

"We'll use a spell similar to the ones that we use to contain a shapeshifter in her human body," Sinead explained to the adepts ringing Seth.

"We'll need more energy than we use to prevent shifters from shifting, as well as a thread of healing from Flora."

"Excuse me," Marion said. "You can prevent shapeshifters from changing forms completely? Without direct control from the Alpha?"

"That's right," Sinead said.

There was no smile on Marion's lips when she looked at Seth now. They were likely thinking the same thing. If preventing shapeshifting was magically possible, then they could save shapeshifter patients from death—patients like Elena Eiderman.

"Why haven't those spells been adapted for medical application?" Seth asked.

"It's too difficult for most witches. People would kill themselves trying to attempt it." Rylie had taken position where the iron-and-stone flooring faded into long grass, which grew all the way to her knees.

"We'd also have to share proprietary sanctuary magic with the public," Sinead added.

"That's not fair," Marion said.

"You're the one who told me we should keep it a secret," Rylie said.

Marion's face fell. "I was?" She must have been wondering if that meant she was responsible for Elena Eiderman's death.

"Let's focus," Sinead said. "Seth, please remove your shirt so we can see what we're working with."

He took a bracing breath, seized the hem of his shirt, and lifted it over his head.

Silence strangled the room.

Seth's decay had gotten worse. It was less grotesque as it advanced because his thorax now looked too inhuman to be properly disturbing, but there was still a hint of the ribcage encasing shadowy memories of the organs he had contained.

Mostly there was light—the glimmer of godly power, which promised to tear away his mortal flesh completely.

When the wound was exposed, he had a harder time shutting off his awareness of the death in the room, too.

One of the witches he didn't know would suffer a brain aneurysm in five years. She would drop dead where she stood with no warning sign.

Two of the witches were going to die in a car accident driving back from Northgate, the town nearest to the sanctuary. Both of them would be drunk. One would remain in intensive care for eight days before succumbing, whereas the other would be crushed to death when the car flipped. They'd take out the driver of the other car in the collision with them.

Nine of the witches would die of old age, over a span of sixty to ninety years—a good life span for preternaturals of their ilk. That indicated they were strong enough to maintain health with magic, but not so strong that the magic would kill them.

Hundreds of students were near enough in the school that he could simultaneously see their lives, too.

He couldn't bring himself to look at Marion. He didn't want to know.

"Do it fast," Seth said hoarsely, eyes fixed on his chest and the smoky power dribbling over his hips.

Sinead began chanting. When she did, the witches raised their hands, linked their fingers, and began to circle him. The spell shoved against his flesh, forcing him into the mold of a human shape so tight that it hurt.

The pain must have showed on his face.

"Careful," Rylie called from outside the circle.

"As careful as we ever are," Sinead said.

The salt ringing the circle of power lifted in a cyclone that whipped at his legs.

Magic squeezed him tighter.

Thread by thread, the fog spilling from Seth's chest retracted. Flakes of skin and bone that had been drifting from the injury reversed.

Getting knitted back together hurt almost as much as when the Hounds had chewed on him. The witches circled and chanted and his skin was growing back together and it *hurt*.

His knees buckled. He sank to the altar with a groan.

The sense of death only grew along with the magic. Threads of life and death pinwheeled through eternity, pulling Seth along with them.

Another of the witches would die while pregnant because her boyfriend shot her in the face.

Yet another would die in childbirth.

A student in the nearest wing was going to die in a dominance fight between werewolves when he was in his fifties.

Another would die of cancer—cancer! Something that nobody had realized that shapeshifters could even get. It would strike her when she was in her eighties and take twenty years to murder her.

And then there was Rylie.

"No," Seth groaned aloud as the magic pushed. "*No.*"

He didn't want to see it. He didn't want to know.

But there was no avoiding it.

He saw the horrible instant that Rylie would permanently shuffle off of the mortal coil.

The magic ended.

Seth came back to reality and collapsed on the altar.

Sinead was kneeling over him, arms folded, a frown on her bow-shaped lips. "We've stopped the degradation."

He looked down. She was right. His skin was no longer flaking away.

"Is he healed?" Rylie asked from outside the circle.

Sinead was silent, so Seth was the one who had to tell them, "No."

Seth was silent for a long time after the coven left with Rylie, sitting alone on the altar. Marion waited to approach. She'd give him all the solitude he needed.

They were at an Academy for educating young preternaturals, and he looked like the most magical thing there. He hadn't pulled his shirt back on, so the wound was still exposed to the air. She caught the occasional glimpse of a heart beating within his ribcage.

Seth must have felt her watching. He patted the altar beside him, silently suggesting that she should sit.

She stood on the ground by his legs, leaned her elbows on the elevated platform, and gazed up at him from below. Marion was tempted to poke her fingers in the gaping wound to find out what that internal fog would feel like. She resisted. It was doubtful Seth would appreciate the intrusion.

"They stopped the degradation," Seth said. "I can tell I'm not dying anymore. But I'm not fixed."

"The problem isn't you. It's with the nature of healing magic." Marion had been able to see the threads of magic as they'd been cast. She had seen its power, and its limitations. "To heal, witches restore a body to its current optimal state. Bones can be mended, but old age can't be fended off. It's only returning people to a template. You have no template."

He glared at the lake behind the ritual space. "Guess that's the bitch about being an avatar instead of a real person."

Marion had seen the term "avatar" in her journals. She'd tried to talk Elise and James into taking on avatars so that they could rejoin the world. She'd even offered to let them crash on her couch once they inhabited mortal bodies—to no avail.

There were many very good reasons that Elise and James only interacted with the world through Marion. One of the reasons—a big one—was that they simply couldn't keep track of anyone else in the mortal worlds.

Gods existed outside of traditional time and space. If they took on avatars, they'd be just as likely to appear five hundred years from now as they would the present. They also might not return in a form that anyone recognized.

It was miraculous that Seth had appeared immediately after Genesis in a body that resembled his old one.

"How do you feel otherwise?" Marion asked. "Do you feel all...murderous?"

"You mean, do I want to kill people? Yeah. I still feel all of that." His head hung between his shoulders. "I know how Rylie dies."

Marion had never heard that much emotion in his voice before. Not even when he'd been dying.

She studied him in the afternoon light that rimmed his bare biceps, his forehead, the rounded bridge of his nose. Despite the wounds, he still looked very young.

And heartbroken.

This wasn't just a mortal avatar of a god. This was a man who'd lived a life before other gods interceded—a man who'd lived and lost and loved.

He still loved, in fact. He was clearly in love with Rylie even though she had cheated on him, had a million children with another man, and now looked like an old lady by comparison.

"How does Rylie die?" Marion asked.

Seth ran his hands over his face. "A phoenix shapeshifter kills her. A woman named Deirdre Tombs."

NINE

Cold shock spread over Marion. "*Deirdre* kills Rylie? Why? When?"

"I don't know exactly when or why. All I know is that this Deirdre Tombs will be the one who pulls the trigger."

"Are you sure? I think the two of them are somewhat friends." Although they may have been the kind of friends where Deirdre was blackmailing Rylie. Perhaps assassination wasn't so far-fetched.

Seth wouldn't meet her eyes. "I'm sure."

After the threats that Deirdre issued in the Winter Court, Marion hadn't needed another confirmation that she was dangerous, but it was sobering to hear anyway. If Deirdre could beat Rylie, then it seemed unlikely that Marion would defeat her in the vote for Konig's title as Prince of the Autumn Court.

Perhaps Konig and Jibril hadn't been wrong to threaten Deirdre with assassination.

"We have to do something to protect Rylie," Marion said.

"Yeah, we should warn her," Seth said.

Marion's thoughts had been so much more murderous that she would have laughed if anything about the situation had been humorous. Even when Seth was becoming a death god, he still wanted to resolve their problems more peacefully than anyone else.

"I heard you're getting married," Seth said.

Marion drew her shoulders in until they nearly touched her ears. "At the end of the week. The marriage only makes sense." She needed him to know. She needed him to *understand*. "Once Konig and I are married, it'll pull the entire Winter Court under Leliel's peace treaty with the Autumn Court."

He was silent.

"It's my responsibility to protect everyone," Marion said. "Did you know that Leliel attacked the Winter Court while we were in Sheol? She killed so many of my refugees. Half of the people I'd tried to relocate to Niflheimr...gone." And those who weren't gone, like Morrighan and Rhiannon and Ymir, were forced to live in a cemetery among the ghosts of those they'd lost.

"So you're marrying Konig because she won't be able to hurt the remaining half."

"And because the wards on the Winter Court

are failing without a sidhe in charge of them. The marriage will allow Konig to bolster the protections on the entire plane."

"What about the part where you're marrying because you love Konig?" Seth asked.

"I do love him," she said. Seth was quiet for so long that Marion's defensiveness choked her. "You don't have a problem with Konig, do you?"

"He's a great fighter," Seth said. "I can see him being a great king, too."

"You've been avoiding me because of my wedding, though," Marion said. It wasn't a question, but another accusation.

He rolled his eyes toward the domed skylight, staring fixedly at the shadowy pattern of branches cast upon the glass. "I've stayed away because I don't want to hurt you, and when we were in Sheol, it was hard to think about anything else."

"You don't feel like that now, though. So it's no longer a factor."

"No, but I told you things about my feelings, about my thoughts—"

"The fact that we have chemistry." Her memories of the Dead Forest were hazy, but she did remember the part where Seth admitted that some kind of feelings existed between them.

"You're getting married."

"I wasn't then."

"You already had a boyfriend. I shouldn't have been saying things like that."

"You'd have said anything to get me away from that door," Marion said. "What's a little bit of a lie between friends?"

Seth raked a hand over his hair, giving a shaky laugh. "Are we friends? Is that what you'd call us?"

"You and I will need to get along for the years to come, so a friendship would be in our best interests." Marion thrust her hand toward him. "Friends?"

"Friends," he agreed. But he still hesitated before shaking.

"In any case, we both understand that our chemistry is due to the fact that you're a god and I'm the Voice of God. The air is clear." Clear enough that she could go ahead and marry her sidhe prince boyfriend for reasons that seemed much less important now that she was with Seth again.

"Sure." He sounded totally unconvincing.

She didn't feel much more convinced than he was.

"Now that the air is clear, I have to be the one to bear bad news," Marion said. "I didn't just lose refugees when Leliel attacked the Winter Court. Charity died too."

Seth's eyes widened. "Charity isn't dead."

"I'm sorry. I know that you and Charity were very good friends, but—"

"No," he said again, more firmly than before. "She's not dead. I told you, I can see everyone's deaths. Charity's still out there somewhere. I can feel the threads of her life."

"Konig told me that Leliel killed her," Marion said. "He was there. He saw everything."

"But she's alive." Seth sounded as sure of that as Konig had been.

"Then why would Konig have told me that Charity's dead?"

Seth stood, snagging his t-shirt off of the altar. He tugged it over his head to conceal the gaping magical hole in his chest. "Good question."

"He was fairly clear about the series of events," Marion said. "Nori corroborated."

Either Konig was confused about what had happened in the Winter Court, or Seth was very, very wrong.

The options seemed to disturb Seth, too. "That means Charity has been missing for a month. I thought she'd have stayed with you. I never would have thought... Jesus."

"I could have told you what I knew—what I thought I knew—if you hadn't avoided me for a month," Marion said.

He looked properly ashamed for the first time. "You're right. I'm sorry."

The door to the ritual space opened. Rylie returned, a golden pendant dangling from one hand. "I have your glamour. Sinead's confident it will conceal your wound."

That was the whole reason that Seth had been waiting. Since they hadn't been able to heal his physical wounds to the point that his body—his avatar—would be indistinguishable than that of any other mortal, he'd planned to hide it.

A man followed Rylie into the ritual space. He was a black man with sympathetic features offsetting the squareness of his jaw and scars plastering one side of his face. He looked like Seth's father rather than brother.

But that was who he was: Abel Wilder, elder brother by a couple of years. A man whose scarring was the result of a pre-Genesis werewolf attack. He was hideous, a monster even in his human form.

He followed Rylie at a distance and didn't approach his brother.

Decades of history hung over them so heavily that it was palpable, even to Marion—the only one in the room who hadn't witnessed what had gone down between them.

From what little Marion knew of Abel, she expected the Alpha werewolf to start throwing punches at the sight of his brother. But Abel only inclined his head in a nod. "Hey."

"Hey," Seth echoed as dispassionately.

Their distant civility made Rylie sigh. "Try the charm on, please."

Seth dropped down from the altar. He took the chain of the glamour from her and donned it.

The change wasn't as severe as when Charity Ballard wore her glamour. Seth only needed to have a single wound healed and it knitted as Marion watched.

"Cool, huh?" asked Abel.

Marion hadn't realized that she'd ended up standing next to the Alpha mate until he spoke. She'd have avoided him if she had. "I suppose."

"The witches here know what they're doing,"

he said. "They're the best."

Only then did she realize he was trying to make her jealous.

She studied Seth's brother. Abel was much taller—nearly six and a half feet, if Marion was any good at such estimations. At least seven inches her superior. Even with his face directed away from her, she made out a sliver of scarring along the bridge of his nose and his chin. If her journals were to be trusted, that scarring would extend all the way to his ear and then down half his chest, as she'd observed during communal swimming time at the lake.

Abel wore the scarring with confidence. He didn't seem bothered by the idea that Marion would see it.

When she returned her attention to Seth, he showed no sign of injury—certainly no scarring near the scale of his brother's. The hole in his chest had been replaced by smooth flesh and rippling abdominal muscle, exposed only because Seth lifted the hem of his shirt to look underneath it.

Every bite that the Hounds had left behind was invisible.

"Amazing," she breathed.

Marion could only assume that Seth had observations as equally non-verbal. Whatever he murmured to Rylie wasn't audible at that distance.

Seth and Rylie embraced tightly. They held on to one another for a long time.

Much too long.

Marion stole another look at Abel. His arms were folded over his chest, but he didn't intervene.

"Your wife seems very close to your brother," she said.

"Mate, not wife. We're not married," Abel said. "And yeah, they used to be close."

"I'm impressed by how copacetic you are about this." Impressed, frustrated—whatever.

"Seth and Rylie have always belonged to each other," Abel said. "I've just borrowed her for twenty years."

"Cuckold," she snarled under her breath.

"What'd you say?"

"Nothing," Marion said louder—loudly enough that she finally caught Seth's attention.

He released Rylie and stepped back. Seth let go of Rylie's hand last, fingers remaining linked until he came to Marion's side.

It appeared all things were forgiven between them.

Marion was almost disappointed when she and Seth left the altar room without so much as a single punch getting thrown.

As soon as they were alone, Seth said, "Time to get to work."

"Work? On what?"

"We have to find Charity," he said, "and your goat-woman. Wanna come?"

Marion checked the time on her phone. An hour. She had an hour before her dress fitting. "Yes, please."

Teleportation remained the fastest method to reach Las Vegas from the shifter sanctuary, but it took Marion ten minutes to talk Seth into using it rather than borrowing Rylie's private jet. She couldn't waste hours on an airplane. He didn't want to phase Marion and make her sick.

Marion won the argument.

They appeared on the roof of the Allure Tower after that.

When Marion regained awareness of her body, she was already done vomiting. Her skin burned as though she'd been struck by lightning and cooked from the inside out.

Seth was watching from a safe distance. "I told you we should have taken the jet."

Marion swallowed wetly, wobbling on hands and knees as she tried to stand. Gods, it had even come out of her nose that time. She was so pretty. Amazing that men ever resisted her charms, with all of the projectile nose-vomiting. "I'll be fine."

"You weren't this bad the first time I phased us to Vegas."

"I think my sensitivity to passing through Sheol is increasing with exposure. But it's fine. I'm fine." She plucked a handkerchief out of her jacket's inner pocket and dabbed at her face. "Thank you for bringing me here. I'll let you search for Charity now." She meant it to be dismissive—a goodbye.

Seth followed her to the rooftop door. "I'm not letting you face Dana McIntyre alone. She's aligned with Elise and James."

"That's a problem?"

"They took your memories and ditched you in the forest," he said. "Who knows what else they might do?"

"The last person to see me before I lost my memory was a goat." That was why she was taking the OPA database information to Dana for analysis. If anyone could determine who the goat-woman was, it would be the well-connected mercenary triadist. "You and your glamour should go back to Rylie. You can frolic in some lovely, sunny fields together while your numerous nephews and nieces chew on your ankles."

She stepped through the door and let it swing closed behind her so quickly that Seth had to reopen it to follow. "Are you mad at me?"

She wondered if he used that innocent tone while murmuring into his ex-fiancée's ear. "I have no reason to be mad at you."

Dana's penthouse was at the top of the tower, so Marion reached it quickly from the roof. Seth caught her before she could knock on Dana's door, turning her gently to face him. "If you want me to go away, just tell me and I'm gone. I promise I don't have the urge to kill you though. Not right now."

That was why he thought she was angry? Because she feared he'd drink her blood again?

"There's nobody I trust with my safety more

than you, and I have access to literal knights for protection these days." Damn it, Marion had a hard time being angry when he looked so regretful. Her thoughts burst from her mouth before she could control herself. "Why have you forgiven Rylie, after everything she did to you?"

"In a few years, after you've been married to Konig for a while, you'll get it."

"You aren't married to Rylie. In fact, Abel isn't married to her either. The two of them *never married*. Doesn't that seem strange?"

"They're mated," Seth said. "Getting married would be redundant."

"Abel says that Rylie belongs to you."

Seth grimaced. "Jesus Christ, Abel."

"Are you guys going to bicker out here all gods-damned day, or are you going to knock?" Dana McIntyre peered through her cracked open door. The chain was still in place. She was holding a sculpted stone piece that was shaped like a flintlock pistol, except that it had no hole for a bullet to pass through. Magic shimmered over its surface.

Marion straightened her jacket as she turned from Seth. "May we enter?"

"He can," Dana said. "You can't."

"I'm not talking to you without her," Seth said.

Dana grumbled obscenities while unlocking her door. When she shut it, released the chain, and opened it wide again, she revealed herself to be wearing full enchanted body armor. Her hair was green on that particular day.

"Get in."

The spellsword's condominium was in disarray. Her weapons had been taken from their tidy mounts on the wall and scattered across every surface. Trash littered the floor.

Marion edged around a pile of laundry so rank it may as well have been circled by cartoon flies. "Where's Penny?"

"Like you care," Dana said. "Look, I have to get to the scene of a crime. The fourth I've had to handle in the last week alone. I don't have time to clean when I'm constantly hunting down demons and performing exorcisms, so stop looking like I need to appear on a reality TV show about hoarders. It's not *that* bad."

"Demonic possessions gone up?" Seth asked.

"You should know. It's your fault." Dana thrust a gauntleted hand toward him. "Phase me to the Linq. Specifically, the tattoo parlor in the back hallway. We can talk while I look over the scene." When Seth didn't take her hand, she gripped his wrist, and then grabbed Marion by the jacket. "Linq. Tattoo parlor. Back hallway. Now."

Reluctantly, Seth snapped his fingers.

Marion smelled brimstone.

She didn't have the opportunity to hit the floor that time, because Dana instantly swept her off of her feet.

"Watch it," Dana said.

She hadn't caught Marion to be nice. She'd caught her because Seth had unintentionally phased them within inches of a massive puddle of blood, at the center of which rested several people who were very obviously dead.

The whole tattoo parlor was covered in blood and death.

Marion clapped a hand over her mouth as her abs tightened. She couldn't tell what would make her vomit first: the teleportation, or the sight of all those bodies.

Dana shoved her toward the wall. "If you're going to barf, do it down your shirt. Don't contaminate the evidence."

Marion managed to swallow the bile down—just barely. There wasn't much left in her stomach.

They were on the far end of a tattoo parlor, which was covered in mirrors, black tile, and posters of an artist's flash. Only some of the available tattoos were visible. The rest had been smeared with runes drawn in blood by hand—human hands. The dead on the floor looked to have carved into their own wrists and throats to produce the medium in which they'd scrawled jagged infernal spells.

Marion was surrounded by blood. Everything was unclean.

She tried to back away, but there was nowhere for her to go. The broken autoclave was dripping. The walls were stained. The chair, the floor—*everything.*

Police were walking around the scene with plastic covering their clothes to keep from getting messy. Marion had no such luxury.

Blank eyes were staring toward her.

"What the hell happened here?" Seth asked, and his voice sounded like it was coming from elsewhere in the casino, as if Marion could barely hear him through several walls. Her vision was swimming.

"Arawn happened," Dana said. "*You* happened."

"Hey! McIntyre!" A woman detective carefully stepped over bodies to approach. "Didn't see you arrive. Glad you're here." She pulled one of her gloves off and shook Dana's hand. "Who do you have consulting this time?"

"Seth Wilder and Marion Garin," Dana said.

The detective had turned to shake hands with Seth and Marion as well, but once Marion's pale blue eyes registered, she picked up on the name too. To her credit, her only sign of shock was going still.

At this point, Marion was becoming as recognizable as any celebutante with a sex tape. Her wedding to Konig was the event of the decade, easily.

"I hope your presence doesn't mean this has to do with gods." The detective finally shook Marion's hand. "Detective Villanueva. Charmaine Villanueva. LVPD preternatural homicide department." It was refreshing to meet law enforcement that wore khakis rather than all black, even if her untailored fashion was rather pedestrian.

"It's an honor to meet you, Detective Villanueva." Marion was unable to muster one of her charming smiles.

Seth shook hands with the detective as well. "So Detective Haskins isn't leading preternatural homicide anymore?"

"Retired. You know him?"

"I'm a former colleague of Brianna Dimaria's."

Detective Villanueva's shoulders relaxed. "Glad to have another of you on board. I don't suppose any of you know what to make of the runes?"

When she gestured at the artist's flash, Marion couldn't help but look again. Her mouth was dry. She still felt nauseous. "These are channeling runes. Someone drew power from these deaths into the Nether Worlds." A hand wrapped around hers. Seth's hand.

When their eyes met, she realized that he wasn't merely offering comfort to her. He was taking it, too.

He was attracted to blood and death. His reaction to the scene of a mass murder was wildly different than hers, but it disturbed him in its own way.

She squeezed his fingers tightly.

"This is Arawn's work." Dana was kneeling by one of the bodies, unworried about her stone armor touching the blood. "He possessed the bodies with demons and dragged the human spirits into the Pit of Souls. More like a meat grinder than a pit, the way he's been doing it."

Marion's knees were weak. "Meat grinder?"

"Look at this." Dana pointed at one of the

bodies. "These cuts are deliberate. They're similar to the last four—aren't they, Detective?"

"Identical." Detective Villanueva swiped through photographs on her tablet and showed them to Seth and Marion. They were starkly lit crime scene images from other casinos.

Marion couldn't focus on them. It wasn't a problem with her contacts.

The smell of blood was so strong.

"The photographers have already been through so feel free to muck around. Let me know when the cleaners can start working. The Linq's on my ass to get this clear ASAP." Detective Villanueva stepped away to talk to uniformed officers on the other side of yellow tape blocking the doors.

Dana remained crouched beside the bodies, boots planted in their blood. She glared at Seth. "Arawn shouldn't be in a position where he's seeking power for ascension. He shouldn't be functioning as a near-god of death with access to the Pit of Souls."

"He killed Nyx." Seth's hand was clamping tighter on Marion's.

"That's not what I'm talking about." Dana straightened. "I found you when I got back to Earth. I told you what you needed to do. What did I say, Seth? I want to hear the words from your mouth."

"Stop it," Marion said softly.

"You told me that Elise wanted me back," Seth said. "She wants me to be God."

"But you're still mortal," Dana said.

"I'm not Elise's toy."

"She didn't elevate you to this level because she's toying with you. She needs someone to responsibly handle the termination of human life and recycling of human souls, and you won't do it, so Arawn's butted in."

"I'm not a killer any more than I'm a toy," he said.

Marion found her ability to speak. "Excuse me, Dana... You've been talking to Elise and James?"

"So what if I have been?" Dana asked.

There was no information in Marion's journals about how to contact the gods, and she hadn't been able to reach out to them ever since having her memories taken away. Despite being the Voice of God, there was very little talking going on.

They were talking to Dana, though.

What if Marion wasn't the Voice of God anymore?

"They want me to be a god?" Seth asked. "I'm not going to trust the people who thought the best way to track me down was to strip an innocent girl of her identity." Even speaking as quietly as he was, ensuring they wouldn't be overheard by police, the vitriol was staggering.

"They didn't plan for the Canope to get broken," Dana said a little more nicely than before. Nice for Dana only meant she wasn't spitting and baring her teeth when she talked. "They never meant for Marion to end up like this...wimpy thing."

Marion stiffened. "Wimpy?"

"Look at you." The scornful tones were back. "The two of you are beyond useless. A god who won't be godly and a mage swooning at the sight of blood."

In her defense, it was a *lot* of blood. It slicked the floor and tattoo chairs in such quantities that it looked like an oil spill.

"Arawn's flooded the Pit of Souls with balefire," Dana said. "Do you know what balefire is?"

"Duat is guarded with it," Seth said.

Marion remembered the contagious fire that needed no accelerant to melt everything it touched. It had been a hideous weapon, truly frightening.

"If it's guarding a city, then it's gotta be watered down. Real balefire, at full force, can't be controlled. A fleck of it would burn through the ground and cut all the way into the Earth's core. It's burning souls right now in the Pit. Some people say it could burn time itself, if you let it run wild long enough." The huntress pushed a body, making it roll over. "These ritual marks are stripping souls for delivery to balefire."

"What's the benefit in that?" Marion asked.

"Laws of physics, bitch. Matter can't get destroyed. It changes. That applies to souls and balefire, too. When balefire breaks shit, there's a massive output of power—and Arawn's going to use that power to ascend to Earth. It'll be the Breaking all over again."

The exact kind of god-level disaster that Deirdre Tombs was attempting to head off with her council.

"Seth needs to take over Sheol," Dana said. "Phase through the balefire. Even diluted, trying to jump through it should kill you."

"Good to know," Seth said. "I won't make that mistake."

Dana rolled her eyes. "Okay. Don't phase through the balefire. Eat a bullet. Whatever. Just *do your fucking job*. Souls shouldn't get burned. Arawn could ruin the whole universe because you're letting him run rampant."

The words "eat a bullet" made Marion cling to Seth tighter. Let Dana think she was wimpy. The woman was talking about Seth sacrificing himself to save people, and that was exactly the kind of noble, selfless act he might be tempted to commit.

It was a relief when he reiterated, "I told you I'm not a killer. I can't run Sheol."

"I pray to the useful gods to save me from the weenie god." Dana kept picking through bodies, measuring their wounds with her fingers, poking through their clothes as if searching for something. "You didn't come to do the smart thing, so you came to me for something else. What do you want this time?"

Marion fumbled to pull out her cell phone. "I tracked down that witness you found for me— Geoff Samuelson. He saw a goat-woman confronting me before I lost my memories. I was wondering if you might know who she was."

"No goats screwed with your head," Dana said. "That was Elise."

The blunt, unsympathetic confirmation of Marion's fears was not making her feel better. "I'm not the Voice anymore, am I?"

"Boo-hoo, poor little Marion. It's hard not being *special*, isn't it? Who's the superior one now? Oh wait. You don't remember that talk. You don't remember why I hate your stupid skinny ass, because you went and *broke your stupid memories*."

"I don't understand," Marion said.

Dana cornered her by the bloody flash. "Elise screwed you up because you weren't listening to her. And before that, you weren't listening to me. I'd been telling you to be careful. That you were going to ruin your life. You know how you responded to me?"

"What did she say?" Seth's voice was surprisingly kind.

"Marion flung her specialness at me. She dismissed me because I'm not Ariane's 'real' daughter, because I'm not Elise's sister, because I'm not the Voice. I'm 'just some fists for hire.' So why should Marion listen to the likes of me?" Dana glared hatred at Marion. "You didn't even come to me and Penny's wedding because you had better things to do."

Marion was numb.

All she could say was, "Oh."

She hadn't written about that in her journals. Apparently the Marion that Dana knew hadn't considered that argument significant enough to write down.

"Marion's changed," Seth said.

Dana snorted. "I didn't get invited to your wedding. I'm still not important enough. So things clearly haven't changed."

"I haven't been involved in invitations. Violet —the Onyx Queen—she's choosing the guest list." But the more Marion talked, the more annoyed Dana looked. "You're right. That's not an excuse. It would be a privilege if you and Penny came to my wedding."

"It's a privilege you're not getting my fist in your face right now," Dana said.

Marion held her phone out, hand wavering. "If you could just look at the list of goat-headed creatures and see if you recognize anyone…"

"Shove it up your ass, princess," Dana said.

"Please," Marion said.

"Gods, you've got some fucking nerve." Dana snatched the phone out of her hand, though. "I'll do it for my curiosity. Not for you. Got it?"

"Thanks so much," Seth said flatly.

He wrapped his arm around Marion's waist and snapped his fingers.

TEN

Marion got sick when Seth took her home to the Winter Court and didn't recover quickly. He could tell that her weakness wasn't because of the brief exposure to Sheol. He was supposed to be Death, after all, and he knew that Marion wasn't dying the way she had been during their visit to the Nether Worlds.

Yet she still didn't rise from where she sat in front of the vanity in her bedroom. She just sat there, immobile, staring blankly at her reflection.

He couldn't leave her like that.

So Seth hung around. There was a lot to see in a magical faerie bedroom. Trees, flowers, furniture that was growing all on its own. It was so humid that condensation gathered on everything, yet nothing became moldy. Marion wouldn't have tolerated the room if it had gotten moldy, even for the sake of being in Niflheimr's warm oasis.

He was walking a loop around the biggest tree in her bedroom when she finally spoke. "You're welcome to explore Niflheimr for the darknet servers, if you want. May your luck be better than mine."

"Don't you want to know what bargain I have with Lucifer over it?"

"You'll tell me if I need to know."

"He said he'd make me a vampire. I could stay in my avatar form as long as I wanted because I'd be undead."

Her eyes lifted, surprised, and their gazes connected through the mirror. "You'd do that?"

"Sinead didn't manage to heal me completely. I don't know what else to do." It wasn't as though killing people was an option for trying to restore his mortal body. "What do you think about vampires?"

"They're the weakest breed. Having you among their number would improve their standing markedly." She toyed with a vase of flowers on her vanity. "What if Dana's right and I'm not the Voice anymore?"

"You're talking to me right now," Seth said, "You're still the Voice of *a* god. Screw Elise and James."

She smiled sadly. "Thank you."

"It's not much of an honor. I am the weenie god."

That actually made her laugh, covering her eyes with a hand. "Oh, Seth." She let her hand fall.

Her pale eyes looked tired. "What's next? How do we find out what happened to Charity?"

"Don't worry about her," Seth said. "I'll figure it out." And he planned to go into Sheol to do it, which meant he wouldn't take Marion, even if she argued with him over it for hours.

Surprisingly, she didn't. "Very well. I was due at a wedding dress fitting ten minutes ago. I'd best catch up."

Seth made a noncommittal noise. It was hard to talk of all the trappings of weddings and not remember his wedding.

Marion didn't seem to relish the subject of weddings any more than he did.

"I have nobody on the guest list," she said. "My mother, Ariane—I haven't been able to reach her. Rylie's invited and will attend, but she's considered a state guest rather than a personal one. Dana is clearly uninterested."

"Nori," Seth said. "Konig."

"They don't count. It's the most important date in my memory, and nobody is coming for me." Marion plucked a flower that was blossoming on the edge of her vanity's mirror, rolling it between her fingers.

"To be fair, your memory doesn't go very far back." He felt guilty trying to joke about it, but he was rewarded with the faintest smile from Marion.

She stood up, stroking the silken petals of the blossom. "You'll come to my wedding, won't you?"

Seth could think of things he wanted to do less than that. For instance, the visit he'd have to make to Sheol soon—he wanted to do that less than attend Marion's wedding. He wanted to die less, too. But other than that...

The idea of sitting in some sprawling sidhe castle while Marion walked down the aisle to meet Konig, one of the biggest blowhards that Seth had ever met, was only more appealing than dying and/or going to Hell.

The fact he didn't respond for so long didn't go unnoticed.

"Aren't we friends, Seth?" Marion asked.

That was an easy answer. "Yeah. We are."

"Why?"

"Well," he said, "I can't seem to shake you off."

Another tiny smile. "I'm the half-sister of the god you hate."

"You fought her off on my behalf before we knew each other. Everything you've suffered is because of me. We're friends, Marion. You're the best friend I have right now."

She handed the flower to him. "I can't imagine getting married without you there."

"I'm not wearing any bridesmaid dresses." Seth tucked the flower over his ear. He could tell he looked goofy thanks to the mirror behind Marion, but now she was actually smiling, and there was even one of those dimples, so it was worth it.

"You'd look pretty if you did."

"Ruggedly pretty."

"That's a yes to my invitation, then."

Seth still didn't answer. He couldn't stop

imagining Marion walking down the aisle just like Rylie had, walking toward him at the altar, while he waited in an uncomfortable tuxedo for his whole life to change.

Rylie had walked away.

"It's the god thing," Seth said. "I don't want anyone to know about it. I've risked enough by showing up at the summit with you. If some guy keeps showing up with the Voice of God..."

Marion's smile melted.

"I'm sorry. I really am. But I have to look for Charity now," Seth said.

She stepped back to grab a voluminous fur cloak from the back of a chair. She flung it around her shoulders. "Please be careful. I'd hate to lose my only friend."

She'd left the room before he even had time to phase out of the Winter Court.

Marion's wedding dress was a lovely thing. That was no shock. It had been made by the sidhe, and their taste in fashion was as incredible as their taste in food. The dressmaker who collaborated with Violet on Marion's gown was a woman named Luciana Sellabon—the same Luciana Sellabon whose cursive "LS" initials were stamped upon fine handbags that cost two years of the average American's income.

With the guidance of a queen with near-supernatural fashion sense, Luciana had outdone herself in producing a dress that would be auctioned for millions after the wedding.

Marion hated it.

"Good, very good," Violet said, walking around her to study the dress from every angle.

They were in a room that had been set aside for wedding staff to use. At the moment, it was filled with mirrors, permitting Marion to see the pins holding the dress at her narrow waist and gathering the hem near her feet. Luciana herself was sitting on a stool by Marion's right knee, pins sticking out of the corner of her mouth as she took notes on changes that needed to be made.

"It's very white," Marion said.

"It's a wedding dress," Violet said.

And what a wedding dress it was. Under her fingertips, the spill of skirts felt like the silk from a spider's spinnerets. It hewed closely to her breasts, mounding them under clawing fractal patterns made of diamonds, which sprayed from the cleft between her breasts all the way up her throat.

The back, on the other hand, was very low, swooping down to show the elegant line of her spine and the dimples above her butt. There were no diamonds there because it would be covered by veils in similar fractal patterns.

Fractals like snowflakes.

That was most likely why she hated it. It made her think of the snowy cold that made the Winter Court hostile.

She was meant to look like the Queen of

Niflheimr. The effect was perfect. And Marion hated it despite the fact that it was, by all metrics, a masterwork of a dress.

It didn't help that she had so much exposed skin, either. She was so *cold*.

"We'll pile your hair atop your head with more of these diamonds." Violet plucked at a thread framing the hollow of Marion's throat. "Your diadem is still being crafted, but it, too, will match. For years to come, when anyone sees you on your throne in that diadem, they'll recall this wedding."

"The event of the decade, just as they've been saying on the news," Nori added helpfully. Her eyes were swimming with tears as she looked at Marion in the dress.

Konig entered. Marion saw him behind her in the mirrors.

"It's not my wedding, but I feel like I should point out that the groom shouldn't see the unfinished product," the dressmaker said. Her voice was as tiny and brittle as her fingers on the dress's hem.

"I don't care about tradition," Konig said. "Out of my way."

Luciana gathered her notebook and stepped aside. Konig leaped onto the platform with Marion, taking her in his hands.

She leaned in for a much-needed kiss, but he wasn't approaching to show affection. He was holding her at arm's length to study the dress with a critical eye that looked very much like his mother's. "We need to see more of your breasts. A sidhe queen would never be this modest."

Marion could already see more of her breasts than she could in a bikini. It was far from modest. "I'm not a sidhe."

"But you will be their queen." He turned her, cool hand sweeping down the line of her spine and lifting shivers in its wake. "The back is fine. I'd like more volume on her ass so it looks like she has actual curves."

"Please, don't hold your opinions back." It was hard to be offended about his remarks on her backside when he was right—she really did have no butt. But it was the best non-butt in all of the Winter Court, she liked to think.

"We are making our debut as king and queen on this day. This is history. Everything needs to be perfect, including this." Konig goosed her.

"Can I get out of the dress now?" Marion directed that to Luciana, but it was Violet who answered.

"Might as well," she said.

A lascivious smile twisted Konig's lips. "Let me help." He reached behind her neck, unclasping the delicate jewels that held the diamond choker in place. He peeled them down and kissed along her collarbone.

At another time, Marion would have welcomed the gesture, even if she'd been avoiding sex with him. She needed to feel needed. Wanted. Even *liked* a little bit. But his mother was watching. Even though Violet was the type to have public orgies on a whim, it was still strange.

Marion leaned away from his lips. "Thank you. I'll let the dressmaker do the rest. I don't want anything damaged."

"Prim, prudish Marion," Konig said.

Nori snorted from the corner.

Marion clenched her teeth. "I need to talk to you, Konig. Ideally it would be a private conversation."

"We're in private," Konig said. Sidhe had very different ideas about privacy than Marion did. There was no point trying to debate that with Konig again, though. He was Marion's match when it came to obstinacy.

"You told me that Charity died when Leliel attacked the Winter Court," she said as quietly as she dared. "Seth says that she's alive."

Konig's face blanked. "You didn't tell me that you saw Seth."

"I'm telling you now," Marion said. "That's beside the point. He told me—"

"Why would you keep that a secret?"

She huffed. "He thinks Charity is alive."

"He's seen her?"

"No, but he can *feel* that she's alive, because he's...you remember what I told you."

"He's mistaken." Konig's violet eyes narrowed in such a way that made it clear he was still hung up on the fact that Marion had seen Seth at all, rather than Seth's claim that Charity was alive. "Where did you meet him?"

"He was with Rylie at the shapeshifter sanctuary," Marion said with a pang of annoyance.

She wasn't sure if the emotion was directed at Konig or Seth. "They used to be engaged. She's now mated to his brother. It's complicated."

"Complicated," Konig echoed, still looking at her a little too hard.

Marion glanced at Violet and Nori in the mirror. They were talking to the dressmaker about some fiddly details on the train. "You're *sure* that Charity died?"

"To be honest, I can't be sure of anything. She was there before Leliel attacked. She wasn't there after Leliel disappeared. After everything that happened... I can only assume." Konig clutched at her hands. "You don't think that Leliel took her, do you?"

Marion couldn't think of any logical reason for the angel to abduct a revenant. If Leliel had planned to run after making her strike, she wouldn't want to be saddled down with a victim.

Violet returned to the couple. "What's taking you so long to remove that? There are other dresses you need to try on."

"I'm only having one wedding," Marion said.

"We'll be hosting a gala the day preceding the event. I've extended invitations to everyone on the council, as we don't have time to lobby for votes unless we bring everyone to us. There's no better way to curry favor than by plying people with unseelie wine."

"You didn't tell me about that," Konig said.

"You're marrying, precious. This is the last thing you should worry about leading up to the happiest day of your life. Don't worry." Her lips spread in a smile that looked ominous along with her blank eyes. "I've got everything under control."

"I don't need your help, Mother."

"Then what's your plan for not being stripped of your title? What have you done to take action, aside from letting your bride-to-be run around Earth on unrelated errands?"

"I was getting votes," Marion said. "I already have Rylie Gresham."

"You'd have had her anyway. You two should be thanking me for giving you the benefit of my experience as queen."

"Just like I should thank you for the benefit of your interior decoration skills?" Konig snapped. "Is there anything you won't control?"

"I can't do anything about how ungrateful you are," Violet said.

Konig flung his hands into the air. "I won't listen to this in *my* palace!"

He slammed the door behind him on the way out.

A crack shivered down one of the mirrors, slicing Marion's white-gowned figure in half.

She wished that she could have stormed after him too, but with the weight of the dress and all its pins, she wouldn't have been able to do anything but hobble pathetically.

No, Marion was stuck with her future mother-in-law.

Violet was serene as her fingers flew over

Marion's bodice, undressing her dispassionately. "Half the job of being a queen is managing our kings. You'll do fine with it. If you can convince everyone that you and my son are a happy couple at the gala, you'll be able to survive anything."

Marion blinked. "We are a happy couple."

"Oh." Violet smiled as she peeled the diamonds away from Marion's shoulders. "Of course you are."

It only took a few minutes to undress her.

Marion shivered in the dressing room while she waited for the next dress to be readied. Luciana and Violet were arguing about which one Marion needed to try on next. Nobody was paying attention to her.

Motion flitted past the mirrors.

It was a familiar small figure—Ymir, whom Marion hadn't been able to pin down for weeks.

She grabbed a robe and ducked behind the mirrors. "Ymir?" she whispered. He was standing against the wall, gazing up at her with big eyes. "What is it?"

He didn't speak. He pointed to his forehead, and hers.

"I don't understand," Marion said, kneeling in front of him.

How had he even gotten into the dressing room? He'd come from the opposite direction of the door, and there were no others that Marion knew of. Yet he had sneaked in without being seen.

Nori called from the other side of the mirrors.

"Marion? Where did you go?"

Ymir jerked away at the sound of Nori's voice. He fled into the shadows.

"Wait!" Marion called.

He vanished.

She tried to follow him, only to realize that he was truly gone. There was a floor tile dislodged, though.

A secret passage.

It would be too narrow for most adults to fit through comfortably, but not too difficult for the little frost giant.

Nori poked her head between the mirrors. "The next dress is ready."

"Coming," Marion said.

She stared hard at that dislodged floor tile, reluctant to leave.

Everyone thought the darknet servers were in the Winter Court, but Marion hadn't been able to find them. They weren't in any of Niflheimr's mapped rooms.

But neither was that passage under the floor.

ELEVEN

The foggy Nether Worlds enveloped Seth in sultry darkness.

He'd appeared in the hive the last time that he visited, so that was where he returned, preferring a familiar destination. The narrow tunnels teemed with demons of all flavors—the ghostly spindles that reminded him of Nyx, creatures that almost passed for human, the insect-like ones with moist eyes rolling atop shiny carapaces.

Just like at the werewolf sanctuary, nobody looked twice at Seth. Teleporting into a public area didn't faze demons. For all they knew, he'd come from some other part of the Nether Worlds.

He found his way past the shops, past Arawn's uninhabited tower, and out into the edge of the hive. From there he could see across the lacework of rivers to the hill where Duat rested, the Bronze

Gates thrusting from murky fog as though it was floating atop it.

The Dead Forest rested between him and Duat.

It was impossible to make out the spikes of the trees among the fog at that distance. He remembered the silence under its canopy, though. He remembered the Hounds hunting him at its edge. It would have been easy to walk into the Dead Forest and let the Hounds find him again. One short stroll, and his mortal body would no longer hold him down. He'd be a god.

That was where the problems could only begin.

Where was Elise? Her presence cast an oppressive shadow over recent events, but the Godslayer hadn't made a personal appearance. She wasn't speaking to Marion. Dana claimed to talk to her, but Dana wasn't without her own agenda. Even Seth, who was on a one-way trip to omnipotence whether he liked it or not, hadn't seen Elise around.

The gods didn't seem to be interested in or capable of interacting with the world directly.

Seth could imagine being in eternity with Elise and James, watching everything happen from a distance, but unable to influence it.

He'd watch Deirdre Tombs assassinate Rylie without the ability to step in, whenever that happened—in the far future, he knew, but how far he did not.

He'd surely be able to see Charity once

omnipotent—whatever had happened to her—but not save her, if saving needed to happen.

He'd watch Marion's wedding to Konig and be unable to reach out.

Or else he just wouldn't care.

Giving up his body wouldn't just be surrendering a body. It would be surrendering his entire life. He'd wanted to help people as a doctor, not retreat to some Mount Olympus and loll with ambrosia while others suffered.

Seth didn't go near the Dead Forest.

He leaped across Mnemosyne and arrived on the grassy banks outside Duat.

He nearly walked right into balefire.

"Jesus," he said, taking a quick step back.

The glimmer he'd thought was the Bronze Gates at a distance was a sheer wall of fire. It was heatless, even just a few feet away, but completely solid. It must not have been true balefire, if what Dana said was true. It encompassed all of Duat without consuming its surroundings. Seth might have been able to walk through it. He wasn't going to risk it.

"Charity?" he muttered at the wall of balefire.

Seth opened his senses enough to feel for the threads of life around him.

It was hard to give into his godly urges after struggling so hard to ignore them. Slowly, his awareness of demons throughout Sheol surged to the surface of his mind, like stars appearing after sunset.

Charity was among them.

Her death was in her past, bright and shining, just as it had been with Lucifer. There would be a death in her future too, but Seth couldn't sense it at the moment.

She was alive.

If he wasn't mistaken, she may have been inside Duat, too.

He walked outside the Bronze Gates, seeking the origin of the balefire. It had sprung from warlock runes the last time he'd seen it. If there was something similar creating this new bubble, then he might be able to tear it down, penetrate it —something that would let him reach Charity.

The sphere was a smooth, solid mass with no obvious spellwork creating it.

There had to be a way inside. He'd spent some length of time in Sheol before substantiating into an avatar and must have been able to control the environment. Seth was a god even if he couldn't remember it.

His gaze tracked across the grassy banks outside Duat toward Mnemosyne again.

They'd lost Marion's memories in Sheol, but Seth's might have still been available for restoration.

He trudged away from the wall of balefire and wavered on the banks of Mnemosyne, knees in the mud, heel of his palm sinking into the damp loam.

With his other hand, he scooped water out of the river. It wasn't cold. It wasn't warm. It felt like touching nothing at all, even though he could see it shimmering in his palm.

"Here goes nothing," he muttered.

He drank.

Memory flitted through him, little fireworks of flashing color that began slowly.

The first of it was the time his mother had locked him in the crawl space under their singlewide, chained up with the spiders. A strange place for memory to start. But perhaps that was where the god had been made: not the moment he'd tumbled, wailing, from between his mother's legs, or in the instant Elise bestowed eternity upon him; it had been when he'd realized that life was as cruel as his mother's cold heart and that he wanted to change it.

He could have done without the memories that followed that one. Unpleasant as it was to be reminded of his now-dead mother, he preferred that to reliving the moment he'd proposed marriage to Rylie Gresham—on one knee in a cattle pasture, while she stared at him in shock.

The first thing out of her mouth after his question had been Abel's name.

Seth remembered the last time they had sex, and how he'd clutched at her with denial, and need, and even a sense of joy he found horrible now, because he hadn't believed that would be the last time.

Since then, nobody had touched Rylie like that but Abel.

Since then, nobody had touched Seth like that at all. Brianna had offered during the week they'd dated, and he'd politely turned her down. There'd been other offers, too—none of them tempting.

Seth's memories skipped from his death before Genesis to waking up in the werewolf sanctuary after Genesis.

It was like every fiber of his being resisted showing him what had come in the gap between.

He scooped more water out of Mnemosyne. He drank.

He *guzzled*.

Nyx was in those dark places.

She had been the first demon Lord of Sheol, stronger than Arawn in her way. She'd been ruling in Hell before it became the Nether Worlds. She'd been Death. And it had worn on her.

Nyx had been happy when Seth sought her out. "You can have it all," she had said, sweeping a hand over the Pit of Souls. "Anything you want."

That had been Seth's Plan A.

He'd thought he could get away from Elise and James by going into the Nether Worlds and taking charge of Death. And he had. Seth had done it for years. Time had a strange flow for gods. Epochs lost in moments, moments stretching to millennia.

That hadn't been enough.

Seth had spent the long heartbeat of Genesis's blackness, when the Nether Worlds and the Pit of Souls had been reformed, learning the ropes of Death alongside Nyx.

He'd hated it. The killing. The dying. Feeling like he wasn't saving anyone.

And then Plan B had come to him: substantiation into an avatar, which meant a return to life, mortality, humanity.

Not before he'd seen how everyone would die, though.

Omnipotence and omnipresence: the twin curses of a god that permitted him to suffuse every moment that had ever been or ever would be.

He saw Rylie dying as though he were standing over her body, because he had been there, in a way.

Rylie was prone, as she'd been so many times when she and Seth had made love together, with all the youthful eagerness that resulted from the discovery of sex's newness. She was no longer young. She was no longer new. And she was not rapt in his arms, but staring blankly at the sky, a hand over her heart, a hole in her forehead.

Deirdre Tombs had instigated this moment. She was braced over Rylie, feet firmly planted in combat boots, curves of her body spilling through tight leather.

She looked grim, but almost as peaceful as Rylie. Her finger remained tensed on the trigger in that instant. There was gunpowder residue on her creamy brown skin. There was blood under her fingernails.

Seth was watching. He saw Rylie's death, and he let it happen.

The woman he'd hoped to marry and be buried alongside once they both died.

He watched her die.

Rylie was already dead, at some point in eternity, and Seth had allowed it.

Lucifer was in the exact same chair at Rock Bottom when Seth returned, as though he'd been waiting there for days. "Made up your mind?" the vampire asked, hunched over the TV. He had a glass of blood on the table. Seth could tell it wasn't synthetic. "You stink like the Nether Worlds, so you must have been thinking it over."

Seth had been thinking it over all right. As soon as he'd shaken off the memories that drinking Mnemosyne had brought over him, he'd walked laps around Duat searching for any way inside. There hadn't been one that he could find.

All the walking in the world couldn't change what he'd learned from that river.

Charity was still missing and Rylie would someday be dead. Seth was unable to address either of those issues at the moment. But he could keep himself from ever being omnipotent again—all-knowing but all-uncaring, watching the woman he loved die without intervention.

"What's it mean, being a vampire?" Seth asked. "How's the hierarchy? The cravings? The symptoms?"

Lucifer turned the volume down on the TV. "Do I have root access to the darknet?"

"Marion said you could have it."

"Great." The vampire slapped a pad of paper on the table. "Write down the login."

Seth squared his shoulders. "She doesn't know where the servers are and wouldn't know how to log in as an administrator even if she did. Other factions have been looking for the servers, though. Marion has only agreed to give them to you."

Lucifer tapped his pen on the edge of the notepad. "Who else is trying to get to the servers?"

"She suspects the angels. The American Gaean Commission for sure. Does it matter?"

"Oh yes. Most certainly. And you don't want those people to have access." He waved down one of the other vampires in his murder and whispered to him. The vampire left after a moment. "I'm going to get you a USB drive with a virus on it. Plug it into the servers and it will do the work."

"What would the others do with administrator access to the servers?" Seth asked.

"I told you that I want them for business," Lucifer said. "Deirdre will want to find criminals and rain swift justice on their heads. Total chaos. The angels, though..."

"They don't want justice, I take it," Seth said.

"Any information worth knowing has passed through the darknet," he said in a low voice. "Some say that there are undiscovered planes parallel to the Middle and Nether Worlds. One of those planes is ethereal."

Seth frowned. "Then why don't the angels nest there?"

"The ethereal plane is supposedly inhabited. Not by people, but by a weapon. A very powerful weapon, which the gods hid during Genesis. There's been speculation about it on the forums. If anyone knows how to get there, it would have been discussed in private messages, which server administrators could read."

"When were you going to tell me you wanted that information?"

"Never, because I don't want it," Lucifer said. "A weapon the gods want to hide isn't worth having. The first Genesis was bad enough." He sucked air between his fangs, making a face as though he tasted something sour. Blood stained his teeth. "What I wouldn't give for a chance to talk to those bastards."

Seth clenched his jaw. "What is the weapon?"

"I've no clue. I don't want to know. That's why you want me to have the servers though—and why you'll want to keep the angels far, far away."

Lucifer's vampire aide returned with the USB drive.

Seth closed his fist around it. "If I get this to the servers, I'm going to delete any information I find about that weapon."

Lucifer rolled his eyes. "That's fine. For all I care, you can do it while I'm draining the last of the blood from your ageless body."

The door to Rock Bottom swung open.

Daylight spilled over the bar, and the responding shouts weren't mere protests from vampires who didn't like the sun. There were shrieks. Cries of pain. And panic.

Tables crashed onto their sides. Chairs slid.

Bodies thumped into each other.

A fight.

Lucifer sighed as he stood, smoothing his hands over his oil-slick hair. "Gentlemen?"

His vampires sitting at the surrounding tables stood, too. "I'll kick them out," said a man with the physical stature of an elephant and the same sickly coloring as Lucifer.

It quickly became obvious that it was no ordinary bar fight, though. Even preternaturals didn't devolve so quickly into blood spilled and lives ended.

The perfume of death cloyed. Seth's mouth was watering, heart beating faster, mind whirling.

People are dying.

Lucifer's murder of vampires swarmed the site of the fighting and Seth drifted past them, silent, unseen, untouched. Everyone seemed to be moving in slow motion to him. He was the shadow of the shadow, drawn by his yearning toward oblivion.

The death was coming from an unexpected place. Not from humans—typically the most vulnerable population in a bar—but from the shifters who had been playing billiards while downing a bottle of pixie vodka.

The humans were the ones doing the killing.

What Seth saw by the pool tables was so strange that his mind was slow to process it, even as his instincts wanted him to move closer, immerse himself in it.

Flaming runes ringed that section of the bar.

They set fire to the walls with inky-sticky smoke and crawled over the flesh of humans. Mortals. Their eyes had gone stark black. Their faces were vacant of sentience.

Demon-possessed.

It took two or three of them crouched over each shifter to kill. Even with the hell-bent drives of someone possessed, which stripped away the normal limits of human strength, they were nothing individually in comparison to a shifter. It took teams to perform a single murder. But murder they did, and it was particularly brutal in the result.

Seth's vision swam from each torn throat to the severed limbs and the puddles of sticky black blood.

"My God," he breathed.

The fact that he had a voice to come from his mortal body was a reminder that he was still a man, even if he were a man eaten from the inside out by immense power.

It shocked him back to reality.

Murder. People were murdering, driven by demons from the Nether Worlds who couldn't physically break onto Earth.

It was Arawn again. He'd followed Seth out of Sheol.

The front door slammed open to reveal harsh daylight as other patrons fled Rock Bottom. This time, when Seth heard the protesting shrieks in response, the tenor of it was completely different.

They weren't complaining because it hurt

their eyes. The demons were complaining because the sunlight burned them, incapable of surviving in the warmth of the sun that their master so longed to bask in. Possessing humans gave them strength to slaughter. But it gave them Arawn's weaknesses, too.

Seth's guns were drawn in a heartbeat. The one he kept in an underarm holster, and the one he kept in his boot.

He moved into the ring of flaming runes.

The possessed were innocent, so he didn't shoot to kill. He shot to disable. With his medical knowledge and perfect accuracy, he struck thighs without hitting the femoral, necks without hitting the air passage or the jugular, hands without breaking any bones.

Unfortunately, when the people fell, they didn't stay down. But they did fall. It gave their victims time to scramble away.

Lucifer was at Seth's shoulder.

"They're dying," the vampire murmured, his voice silken promise. "It's too late to save them. They're already soulless. Can't you feel the emptiness?"

That didn't stop Seth from sweeping in to stop the violence. Despite a decade as a doctor, he was still a werewolf hunter at his core.

He pinned down possessed ones thrashing with bloody wounds. He pushed victims away. He shouted to the crowd, "Run! Leave the door open, but run!"

And when they obeyed him, they left Rock

Bottom flooded with sunlight from outside.

Where the harsh rays directly contacted possessed flesh, there was smoke. Screaming. Pain.

Seth seized the nearest of the possessed mortals and slammed her into the floor. "Who's your master?"

She smiled through the pain. Her body bucked under him, agonized, but still she *smiled*. "You know who I am." Her voice was deep, masculine.

"What the hell do you think you're doing, Arawn?" Seth asked. "Don't you realize what burning up all these souls are going to do?"

"They'll give me the strength to go after your girlfriend's wedding," Arawn said through the woman.

Anger surged in Seth. "Whatever grudge you've got against me for screwing up your plans in the Nether Worlds... God, don't take it out on her. Take it out on *me*."

"Hurting them is the second-best way to take it out on you since I haven't reached Marion. Yet." The woman's eyes blanked under him. He felt the instant that her body died. Arawn's demon vanished from her, and she went limp.

The deaths spread through Rock Bottom like a wave. It struck those nearest to Seth first, and then those beyond the billiard tables next, and then those nearest the walls.

Every single mortal who had been in the bar was dead instantaneously. Even when Arawn vacated them, his presence hung like a dark cloud over Rock Bottom.

Seth struggled to his feet, burning with hatred at his core.

So many deaths. So many people succumbing to a casual sweep of Arawn's hand.

The demon's disembodied voice whispered through Rock Bottom.

Their souls will feed me, he said.

Seth gawked as smoky wisps lifted from the bodies of the dead. Not all of the souls had been scraped out of those mortal vessels during the possession. Some lingered.

And he wanted them.

Seth had never taken a soul before. The only time he'd taken blood had been from Marion's throat when she'd been dying, and that terrible act had been committed out of mind, out of body, when he'd been struggling to rescue her spirit.

Yet it was easy to visualize gathering all those souls, all those *humans*, and walking them to death. He could spare them from the balefire in the Pit of Souls. He could save every last one of them.

"Do it," Lucifer urged, eyes bright with hunger, blood staining his lips rose-crimson. "Take their souls."

All Seth could bring himself to say was, "No."

Arawn's shadow descended.

The demon inhaled the souls, and they were gone.

TWELVE

Nori called Marion using their statuettes while she was poring over maps in her bedroom. "The Onyx Queen wants you." Nori's voice seemed to come directly out of the tiny white soapstone figure.

"Now isn't the best time." Marion flicked the statuette so that it fell over on her desk. "I'm busy."

"It's for the counseling."

Marion swore internally. She'd forgotten about the pre-wedding counseling she'd agreed to share with Konig. It was sidhe tradition for the parents of those to be married to instruct their adult children in the ways of marriage. Since Marion had one dead parent and one who didn't wish to be in touch, the responsibility fell on Rage and Violet alone.

If given the choice, Marion would have preferred to be eaten by Hounds again rather than talk marriage with her in-laws.

"I'll be right there," she said, stuffing the statuette into her pocket.

Marion shoved the maps of Niflheimr into one of her drawers. She had been searching for empty spots where secret passages could be hidden. Finding the darknet servers for Seth was more important than the counseling, but not as urgent.

All decorations that had yet to find purpose were collected in Violet's chambers, as though the wedding had vomited all over the expansive in-law quarters. Konig sat among a field of enchanted red flowers, looking as annoyed as Marion felt.

"I hope your days have been going better than mine," Konig muttered. They hadn't gotten a chance to speak about what had happened during Marion's visit to Earth. In fact, the only talk they'd shared was about Marion's flat butt and Charity Ballard.

She wiggled onto the narrow strip of couch beside him. "Not unless you think that Arawn murdering people all over Earth to prepare his assault against our wedding is 'better.'"

"Oh, is that what he's up to? Good thing we're here dealing with petty formalities instead of preparing for battle with a demon, then."

"An army needs a unified front." Violet breezed into the room. She was dressed in her idea of casual, which meant a few less pearls in her hair, though she was still draped in enough jewels to buy a small country. She descended onto the couch opposite Konig.

"Are we waiting for Rage?" Marion asked.

"He can't come today," Violet said. "I've done the traditional counseling for many a parentless couple, though. I'll have no trouble talking the two of you through this on my own."

"This is stupid, Mother," Konig said. "You can't call something tradition when we've been doing it for less than a generation."

"How are traditions forged?" Violet asked. "Where do they come from?"

"Decades of practice, doing what our foremothers did."

"We don't have foremothers. Until Genesis, our breed didn't exist. We'd been eradicated." Violet dug her fingernails into the soft billows of her skirt. "By the angels."

Marion ducked her head, unable to meet Violet's eyes. "By my father, Metaraon." The first Voice of God, whose machinations had ultimately led to the shattering of the entire world.

Violet's response was unexpectedly tender, though the blankness of her eyes made her look cruel, even when she spoke gently. "Don't feel guilty. You're not responsible for what he did—only what *you* do. You're shouldering your role in the healing. It's fitting that this union should happen at this time." Her words went sharp. "But not until you've been counseled."

"If it was that important, my dad would be here," Konig said.

"Rage is where he needs to be," Violet said. "Tell me what marriage means to both of you.

Konig first, darling."

He clutched Marion's hand, squeezing her knuckles with the irritation he couldn't take out on his mother. "It's an alliance."

"Marion?"

"I agree with Konig," Marion said. "It's a lifelong alliance, joining our might into a single unit." Konig and Marion had never agreed on anything with more confidence than that.

"You do realize that Konig will benefit from this more than you, don't you?" Violet asked. "The line of succession is matrilineal. If Rage and I had produced a daughter, she'd be next in line for the throne. As it stands, Konig will never rule unless he marries a woman."

"I didn't know there was a line of succession at all. Why didn't anyone get Niflheimr?"

"The queen had no female relatives to receive control," Violet said. "She and her husband never produced children at all."

Marion gave Konig a sideways look. He would never rule unless he married. That was probably something she'd known before losing her memories, but it came as a surprise now.

He was too busy looking sullen to notice Marion's expression.

"Nevertheless, our alliance benefits both of us equally," Marion finally said. "I can't hold Niflheimr at all without a sidhe to take over the Winter Court's magic."

"You'll have to live alongside one another for the rest of your mortal lives, and that requires a much sturdier foundation than merely united goals. The sidhe's veins flow with love and sex, irreversibly intertwined. Did you know that, Marion?"

She was startled—and a little embarrassed—to be singled out by the queen in this. So her response was more honest than she'd have planned if given time to consider it. "You have orgies with total strangers."

"Not all love is that of husband and wife," Violet said. "There is love of friends, love of body, love of life. It's all equal. Sidhe must marry for love too."

"Says the woman who's screwed virtually every faerie in her court," Konig said.

"With your father's consent and often his participation."

"How much of this counseling is going to involve TMI about sex lives?" Marion asked.

Konig and Violet gave her identical blank looks.

To them, there was nothing TMI about sexual affairs. Even if the people discussing it were related by blood.

"Never mind," Marion said.

"What do you want out of this marriage?" Violet asked her. "We already know about the alliance, so please think about your emotional needs, and your long-term personal goals."

Marion hadn't given very much thought to anything beyond survival. She spoke slowly while her mind struggled to produce a satisfactory answer. "I think...I want...someone who will take care of me?"

Konig laughed. "Take care of *you*? You're the last person in the world who needs anyone to care for you, princess."

"I suppose." It didn't seem like a fair question. Knowing what she'd want from marriage was too advanced for a relationship that felt barely weeks old.

"I want a beautiful woman who will be my mental, physical, and political match," Konig said without hesitation. He'd had much more time to contemplate the relationship. "I want a marriage for the history books."

"I already know what *you* want," Violet said. "I'm speaking to your bride."

Marion gazed at Konig's perfect face, his tousled hair, the shards of his purple eyes. They were certainly well matched in beauty, the two of them. For every woman who couldn't breathe at the sight of Konig, there was a man who would lose his footing at a mere glimpse of Marion.

That didn't matter to her.

"I can give myself anything I want," Marion said. "I can get money or power of all persuasions. I can fight my own enemies. I can run this palace. Were I to spend my entire life alone, I would be fine. On the other hand, relief from the unrelenting pressure is something nobody can give me except you. Just to feel as though I'm not always in control—to be cared for, and sometimes permitted not to be responsible for everything—

would be priceless."

Konig laughed again, and each chuckle felt like a needle in her heart. "Marion, princess, you're the Voice of God. You don't get a break. That's not what you're here for."

"I'd like the feeling, though. Perhaps it makes me a poor feminist, wanting a man to be in charge..."

Violet leaned forward to pat her hand. "The most radical feminist act is for a woman to be true to herself."

"Well, don't you worry your pretty little head about any of that," Konig said. "I've no trouble being in charge of everything. I know your limitations better than you do."

"I don't have limitations," Marion said. "I *can* do anything."

"Listen to what you're saying. You're contradicting yourself left and right." He dropped a kiss on her shoulder. "Are we done here? Have we fulfilled our traditional responsibility to marital counseling now that we've talked about our *feelings*? Because there are more constructive uses of my time."

"We should talk about the physical elements of marriage," Violet said.

Marion swung from feeling put-off by Konig's abruptness to agreeing with him passionately. Talking about the "physical elements" must have meant sex, and that was absolutely not something she would discuss in that company.

She stood. Konig did too. Violet watched them

with empty eyes and an unreadable expression.

"Party starts tonight." Konig swatted Marion's butt. "Get yourself pretty. We need to make a good show."

He was gone before Marion could say a word.

"My son's not the most sensitive, but he's illustrated one important thing for a queen and wife to know," Violet said. "They need us to look strong, even when we're not. We're the ones who run the kingdom. The house. The children eventually. And we have to do it while pretending that they're the ones in charge." Her shoulders sagged. "It's okay to feel weak, as long as you don't act weak. It's a performance that never ends."

Marion hesitated with a hand on the door. "Are you performing?"

"Always," Violet said softly. "Always."

Hours before the time of the gala arrived, the Onyx Queen finished transforming Niflheimr from the miserable site of tragedy into a shimmering mecca of pleasure. The holes in the palace had been repaired or concealed with flowers. Steel flowed among the vines, creating lattice upon which magical flora could bloom, filling every one of the dark ice hallways with blossoms that glowed from the inside.

It wasn't quite on the level of the magic that allowed a jungle to grow in Marion's bedroom, but

Violet hadn't wanted to totally mask the natural beauty of the Winter Court. She'd wanted to augment it.

Now the council was arriving to enjoy it all.

Marion met the guests on the balcony where planeswalkers and sidhe brought the politicians in. She wore a single fur-lined cloak that wouldn't make her look as susceptible to the cold as she felt.

Underneath, Marion wore one of the many dresses that Luciana Sellabon had created for her. This one was red with nearly orange undertones—a color very much typical of the Autumn Court. It curved over her breasts and pinched at the waist, giving the illusion of longer legs. It was the dress of a princess waiting to become queen, like a rosebud hours from blooming.

Konig matched her, she knew. He wore robes in the same shades of velvety red with leather leggings and boots that made him a foot taller than Marion. He looked like rock star royalty, young and sexy but traditional.

He was elsewhere, though, leaving Marion to handle the greeting with none but a handful of the Raven Knights to guard her. They'd been dressed in tones of cold blue that matched Niflheimr, as Marion and Konig's personal guards soon would.

The sidhe were forced to tone down their magic for the sake of the arriving party members, many of who were mortal. Even without the distorting vibrancy of sidhe energy, though, all of Niflheimr and its inhabitants—especially the Raven Knights—were so resplendent that it made

Marion's eyes ache in their sockets.

"Thank you for coming," Marion said, shaking hands with Ruelle Myön, the High Priestess of the Allied Covens.

"It's my pleasure." Ruelle's hungry eyes drank in the staircase behind Marion. Covetous fantasies skimmed the surface of her mind. Ruelle hadn't come to have her mind changed about the vote—she'd come to have sex with unseelie sidhe, and she couldn't wait to dig in.

Marion ordinarily made no attempts to read minds, but she reached into Ruelle's to see what she'd already decided about the vote.

Her heart skipped a beat to see that Ruelle would vote against Konig.

Perhaps there was something to be done about that. Ruelle was singularly focused on sex with the sidhe, and it wasn't like the sidhe were unwilling participants. Marion would ask Konig if they could bribe Ruelle with a member of their court.

Marion shook hands and exchanged light kisses with Ruelle's entourage. In addition to bringing her coven—all twelve of them—she'd brought a few heads of other covens. There was more than enough space to accommodate them. Most seemed as excited about the festivities as Ruelle.

"Please see them escorted to their rooms," she told one of the Knights. He bowed in acquiescence. Ruelle's mind bubbled with glee.

The ley lines shimmered. Adàn Pedregon from *Los Cambiaformas Internacional* appeared flanked by a pair of planeswalkers—men clad in enough leather that they passed for unseelie, though they lacked the symmetric beauty. They were likelier human witches, and bodyguards, judging by their deliberate movements.

One at a time, others from his organization appeared. They were golden-eyed shifters decked out in French and Italian couture, including many designers that Marion recognized. They were her kind of people.

She shook hands with each of them in turn as well. It was impossible to get a sense of their breeds, but when she lightly probed their minds, she sensed a lot of feathers and hooves. Most werewolves went to Rylie. Adàn was accompanied by other types of shifters.

Marion greeted Adàn last with a kiss on each of his grizzled cheeks. "Thank you for coming. It's an honor."

"The honor is mine," he said with a thick Spanish accent. Polite as the words were, his tone was not. Nor was it hostile. It was...cautious.

"I hope your journey was uneventful," Marion said.

"It was quiet enough," Adàn said. "We are rested for events to come."

Instinct tugged at Marion. Rather than having the Knights take charge, she said, "Please, let me escort you to your room."

"Thank you," he said, offering his arm to her.

Marion and Adàn headed into the tower, trailed by his people. Adàn's movements made it clear that he was a stag shifter—a hart—even when he was on two legs. He was slow, purposeful, graceful. He felt as solid as a stag under Marion's hand, too. His arm hair was coarse on her fingers.

"How are the gods doing?" Adàn asked.

Marion had no clue. "They're gods," she said with a shrug.

"Lie to me," he said. "Tell me they writhe in a hell of their own making for what they did in Genesis."

Her stomach lurched. "I can tell you anything you want to hear. It won't make it true."

"Then tell me you'll punch them in the face next time you're speaking."

He might have been joking—it was hard to tell. But the whole line of conversation made Marion deeply uncomfortable.

Seth feared being outed as a god for good reason. Too many people had lost loved ones in Genesis—Adàn Pedregon among them, according to the file Marion had read about him. He'd lost all of his adult children, and at least two grandchildren.

Most of those people would love to have a figure to lash out at. Few of them were quite as powerful as Adàn, though.

Marion changed subjects as they moved downstairs. "Your party has been given rooms near the ballroom to ensure you have convenient access to the festivities. The rooms have been enchanted to prevent the noise from disturbing you, though."

"Forget the niceties. I have no interest in small talk." He surprised her by speaking in French—the language that Marion had spoken with her mother as a child, and which she remained fluent in.

"Very well," she responded in kind. "I feel much the same."

"I know why the Onyx Queen has thrown this exclusive pre-party for the speakers. This is an attempt at coercing votes. I'm only attending because my men can use the respite. When it comes to the vote, I prefer to be civilized and negotiate openly."

"What do you want in exchange for your vote?" Marion asked.

"I want a route through the Ethereal Levant," Adàn said.

He was one of the only speakers who had voted to give the Winter Court to angels at the summit, so the news was no surprise. Adàn and LCI inhabited Western Europe; opening a path through the preternatural no-man's-land known as the Ethereal Levant would permit access to Africa.

"A path sanctioned by angels wouldn't do anything about the demons outside the EL and in the Sahara," Marion said.

"I haven't asked you to do anything with the demons. I merely want the angels to give us free travel through their territory. Arrange it for me and you'll have my vote."

"That can be done," Marion said. "I'll speak

with Jibril. If he agrees, I'll need you to speak on my behalf with your cohorts before the vote, too."

"Excellent. Then it's settled."

The relief was overwhelming. Marion had a vote—one person on her side other than a reluctant Rylie Gresham. If LCI went her way, then the Allied Covens may follow, as well as the Oceania Witches. They were all on good terms.

Optimistically, she could have as many as six votes, including herself and Konig.

Her relief was short-lived. She approached the hallway with Adàn Pedregon's assigned rooms and found Deirdre Tombs walking from the other direction. Everyone else had dressed up for the events, but Deirdre hadn't bothered. She still wore her usual leather everything.

Jolene Chang looked equally disinterested in the bacchanalian festivities to come. She smiled toothily when she saw Marion, exposing the needle-like fangs in her jaws.

"Here you are, sir," Marion said.

"Thank you." Adàn gave her a short bow and stepped into his rooms, accompanied by the planeswalkers.

His door shut.

Marion directed the rest of the people to their rooms, and they were soon gone, too. Deirdre and Jolene lingered until they were the last in the hallway. The silence between them was especially awkward with the music already thrumming from the ballroom, echoing through the halls and making the floor vibrate.

It was surprising that the guards let Jolene Chang back into Niflheimr after her attempts to sneak off the last time. Violet must have approved her as a guest. She had more faith in the American Gaean Commission's behavior than Marion did.

"Are you looking for the party?" Marion asked. Internally, she wondered, *Or looking to kill Rylie?*

"We've already been in the ballroom," Jolene lisped around her fangs. "Nothing there for us."

"Wine, music, dinner, dancing..."

"Nothing," Deirdre said. "What's Adàn want from you? How are you going to bribe him into siding with your cause?"

Marion recoiled. "I'm not bribing anyone."

"Wine, music, dinner, dancing," Jolene echoed.

"Not bribery at all," Deirdre agreed. She strode down the hall past Marion, heels clicking on the floor. "Come on, Jo. Let's go to our room to rest. It's going to be a very long couple of days."

THIRTEEN

Of all of Violet's outstanding work, the ballroom was the most impressive. She'd polished cog-work suspended from the lifted ceilings, caught between the rafters like insects in spider webs. Specks of light captured in frosted bubbles drifted in clusters so dense that they nearly looked like clouds, which even snowed actual soft snowflakes, oversized to show their unique shapes. She'd taken care that the snow evaporated before hitting the ground, just as she'd ensured the temperature was a comfortable eighteen degrees near the floor.

It was especially impressive how Violet had managed to tone down the sidhe magic's distortion to something palatable to visitors. The room swirled every time Marion turned her head, giving an aura of the surreal without being overwhelming.

Of course, Violet was used to entertaining political guests in the sidhe courts. Bribing them, Deirdre might say.

Konig was near the orchestra. The naked musicians were coiled around handcrafted instruments and the motions of their delicate fingers on the strings was a promise of how they would play their lovers later that night.

"How are things going, princess?" Konig gave Marion a hand to help her mount the stairs to the stage.

Marion felt too dressed around the orchestra. "Everyone's here," she said, handing him a flute of cordial. "So we have that going for us."

She'd greeted many of the factions personally, and she had seen most of the people who now filled the ballroom. Chances were good she'd met many of them before too. It looked like the hostile ice prison she was trying to make home was filled with strangers, though—all of whom were far too interested in looking at Marion. She was literally on a stage to be stared at.

Why did it bother her so much? This was what she'd wanted. The attention. The recognition. The prestige.

Marion felt queasy.

With a shimmering chime, wind stirred around them, tossing Marion's curls and flashing her calves under her skirt.

The angel Jibril appeared among the fake clouds clinging to the rafters.

He dropped to the stage beside them.

"Speaker," he said, bowing to Marion. Then he turned to Konig. "Your Highness." Jibril was wearing a slim-cut black suit instead of his usual gray-toned robes. It didn't have a tie or vest, as was modern fashion among humans, so he looked passably mortal.

"Everyone's supposed to come through the main entrance on the balcony," Konig said, frowning. "You shouldn't even be capable of jumping through other ley lines like that."

"No, I shouldn't," Jibril said.

It was his way of quietly warning Marion that the wards were still growing weaker.

"Thank you for coming," she said.

He gave another half-bow. "I wouldn't miss the festivities." Quieter, he added, "Have you been speaking with the other members of the council."

Konig swirled the cordial under his nose, inhaling deeply. "I had an interesting talk with the Australian witches. They seem inclined to support us."

"Same with *Los Cambiaformas Internacional*," Marion said. "Adàn Pedregon wants a safe travel route through the Ethereal Levant before he'll agree to vote for us, though. Jibril, do you think we can arrange that?"

The angel folded his hands behind his back, gazing out over the crowd. Adàn and his shifters were along the wall where food was being served. Shapeshifting required enormous energy, so shifters were always eating.

"I don't see how that would benefit us," Jibril

said.

"You'd have my good will," Marion said.

"You said I'd have that if I officiated your wedding, too. This is as far as our show of peace goes." Jibril's tone bordered on hostile.

Marion felt Adàn's vote slipping away from her. "There must be something we could do."

"Protection," Jibril said. "Your mage craft is more advanced than anything we have at the College in Dilmun. You could give us the spells we need to close the door to the Nether Worlds that allow demons to attack our city."

"I could, if..." Marion bit the inside of her cheek. "My memory, you see. It's still a problem."

"You'll come to the College, though," Jibril said. "You'll try to help us piece together the mage craft."

"I can promise to try, but I can't promise results."

"It would be enough. Agree to come to Dilmun and you'll have Adàn Pedregon's path through the Levant."

"Done," Konig said without hesitation.

Jibril didn't often smile, so when he did, it was more than a little unsettling. "The appetizers look delicious. I'd like to get some before they're all gone." He bowed to them one more time before dropping gracefully off the edge of the stage, leaving nothing but a few downy feathers at Marion's feet.

"I can't go to Dilmun," Marion whispered to Konig. "The wards will fail the rest of the way if I keep leaving. I don't know they'd survive even one more trip out of the Winter Court."

"But we are about to get married. Don't worry, you pretty thing. I'll take care of it all." Konig lowered his lips to her throat, kissing her gently. He'd been more careful about such gestures of affection lately. Trying to respect Marion's boundaries, she suspected. But now was the time to put on a good show—to look like a couple who deserved to marry, and whose titles no decent person would strip.

Nori stepped into the center of the ballroom, drawing all eyes to her. "Your attention, please." Her nervous voice was too small to project throughout the ballroom, but the knot of magic glittering at her throat took care of that. "Thank you all for joining us to celebrate the union between Marion Garin, the Voice of God, and Prince ErlKonig of the Autumn Court."

Everyone applauded politely, and Marion and Konig kissed again. Long enough to show affection, but not so long as to be indecent by non-sidhe standards.

Even with her eyes closed, Marion could feel the weight of the Onyx Queen's stare.

If you can convince everyone that you and my son are a happy couple at the gala, you'll be able to survive anything, Violet had said.

And Marion had protested, *We are a happy couple.*

Nori explained where the guests would be able to find the amenities. She encouraged people to ask for help from any of the servants or even the Raven Knights, who ringed the ballroom.

Then she said that Konig and Marion were going to initiate the festivities by leading a dance. Marion had expected this. She'd suggested it, in fact.

"A dance?" Konig extended his hand toward her.

Marion couldn't hesitate to accept. This was her event—not Violet's—and this was her kingdom and life at stake.

She drained her flute of cordial and set it on a tray. Liquid courage. "It would be my pleasure."

Magical light shined on them in a shimmering veil as he led her onto the dance floor. The crowd parted like waves of an ocean to let them pass. Marion took inventory of the faces she knew as Konig guided her toward the center of the room.

Violet was there, but her husband was not, as he had to attend to the matters of the Autumn Court.

Adàn Pedregon and his planeswalkers were there.

So were Deirdre Tombs and Jolene Chang.

The face that surprised Marion the most was Rylie Gresham's, all round and pale. The Alpha was wearing a simple golden sheath that wasn't much fancier than her usual skirt suits. Marion had to admit that she looked lovely with her hair brushed out like that, and with delicate bangles on her wrist. It was easy to see why Seth would have fallen in love with her, plain as she was.

Konig twirled Marion, breaking her attention from Rylie.

There had been time for brief dancing lessons in the last few weeks, preparing for the reception that would follow the ceremony. Marion hadn't really needed it. Her body remembered dancing the way it had remembered doing archery.

She eased into ballroom-style dancing effortlessly, arms framing Konig's, chin lifted.

"Relax," Konig said when he pulled her in an arc back against his chest again. They swayed together. "You look like you're waiting for a funeral."

It took conscious effort to relax her features into a smile. "Do I?"

"You're not nervous, are you?"

Marion's laugh was a little too high-pitched to be convincing. "I don't get nervous."

"You didn't use to." Konig led her with a hand spread across the small of her back, his movements swift and sure. "You're not who you used to be, though." He said the second part with his lips close enough to hers that she tasted the cordial on his breath.

"I'm doing what I can, but I feel like a fraud."

"I love you, princess," he said. "I love *you*. You're still my princess. You still own every single person watching us, and even if you've forgotten that, I haven't." He spun her so that her back pressed to his chest, and his lips touched her temple. "You look exceptionally beautiful tonight."

When she smiled this time, it was genuine. "It's hard to imagine that I used to handle these situations with confidence."

"Think less and enjoy more. It's the sidhe way." When he spun her again, he caught a goblet from a server and offered it to her. This was not cordial, but wine, rich and heady.

If Konig was good at anything, it was dancing. He'd told her recently that his father used to be what Konig described as a "rock god," and he'd grown up in a household with music throbbing at its heart. His body showed familiarity with the orchestra's thumping strains, accompanied by massive drums and even a couple of electric guitars.

He wasn't a classically trained dancer, but he had such charisma that he didn't need to be.

By the time the first song ended, Marion was actually enjoying herself.

They were joined by others for the second song, and the third. The more that Marion smiled and laughed, the more people seemed willing to join in.

She really did own them all.

It was during the fifth song—or the sixth?—that Nori appeared beside them, head low, hands clasped.

"May I have a moment of your time, Prince?" she asked. "Sorry, Marion."

Marion broke away from Konig. She had actually worked up a little bit of a sweat, which she hadn't thought possible in the Winter Court.

"Business calls?"

"Always, I'm afraid," Nori said.

"I won't be long," Konig said, kissing Marion.

Whether it was the wine, the music, or the confidence Konig shared with her, Marion felt emboldened. She didn't let him pull away. She grabbed a fistful of his long black hair and kissed him harder.

There was fire in his eyes when she finally let him go.

"Princess," he murmured, brushing his thumb along her jawline. "You tease."

Then Konig left with Nori. Marion was alone on the dance floor.

Rylie appeared beside her. "You look disappointed. Want to dance?"

"No thank you," Marion said coolly. "Kind of you to think of me, though."

A male waiter dressed as minimally as his female counterparts passed them. Patterns of frost barely concealed his manhood. Marion blushed hot as she grabbed a fresh glass of wine.

She wished it had been a Long Island Iced Tea.

"You've done well with the ballroom," Rylie said.

"It's the work of my mother-in-law," Marion said. "I'm not allowed to make decisions surrounding my wedding."

"It's your life," the Alpha said. "Don't let others control you."

"With all due respect, I'd prefer not to have this conversation with you," Marion said. "At least my mother-in-law probably doesn't have a contingency plan for murdering me. The sidhe respect me."

Shock widened Rylie's eyes. "Marion, I—" And then the shock turned to blankness.

She was looking at something over Marion's shoulder.

Marion turned.

Even though the snow-fogged ballroom was packed with politicians and their assistants, one person in particular leaped out to Marion among all the rest. It wasn't just because the man wasn't dressed for a formal occasion in a black t-shirt and Carhartts.

Seth joined Marion and Rylie. He wasn't wearing his under-the-shoulder rig, but Marion peeked behind him, and the bulge at the small of his back confirmed that he was armed.

It wasn't a social visit.

"We need to talk," Seth said.

Rylie ran her fingers through her hair, straightening imagined tangles. "Of course."

"No, sorry," he said. "I'm talking to Marion." He offered a hand to her. "Do you want to dance?"

Behind the orchestra at the head of the ballroom, veils sectioned sound equipment from the rest of the party. Even magical equipment still needed cabling, speakers, and lights, and veils had been less resource intensive than a glamour spell to hide them.

That was where Konig dragged Nori, pinning her against a speaker as he kissed her.

Nori tasted more like burnt grass than oak like Marion did. But with his eyes closed, he could imagine she was Marion. He could imagine that he was getting revenge against his fiancée by pressing forcefully against Nori's body, feeling all the places that Marion wouldn't allow Konig to touch.

Marion had been showing her perfect body off, flashing the majesty of her ethereal power, and even kissing him...but refusing sex. For weeks. *Months.*

She had to know what it was doing to him. It must have been a deliberate play to torture him.

Marion had lost her memory, but she hadn't really changed.

Konig had selected Nori's dress for this occasion, making sure that the slit rode high enough on her thigh that he could get access without needing to strip her. The bodice, likewise, was loose enough that his hands could slip inside.

His fingers caressed her. She sighed.

"I really do want to talk to you," Nori gasped against his neck, clinging to his shoulders. "It's—oh, *Konig*—"

"Quiet." He pressed his hand over her mouth. "We're barely concealed back here. We don't want to be found."

The danger of it must have thrilled her because she groaned under his palm.

Konig made use of Nori quickly, though not without compassion for how aroused she would be under his ministrations. It had quickly become obvious that Nori was addicted to the sensual magic of the unseelie. She loved every instant that he touched her, was inside her. And he knew her body well enough to bring her to the point of ecstasy within minutes, while still satisfying himself.

He wasn't selfish or selfless. The sidhe knew that sex was best when all came away satisfied.

And they did.

Konig put Nori's dress and hair to rights while she was still slumped, panting, atop the speaker. "Now tell me what you wanted to say."

"Deirdre Tombs," Nori said. "I found information on her, like you wanted me to."

"You've got my attention."

"She used to be a terrorist. She was affiliated with a shifter who killed hundreds of innocent people a few years ago—do you remember the elections for Alpha? The opposition?"

"Everton Stark, yes. Deirdre Tombs was his Beta. There was scandal about her rise in politics after that, but she's been clean ever since. She's considered redeemed."

"Then why does she spend three months a year in South Africa, visiting a property owned by the Stark family? She goes out of her way to conceal her travel plans. People aren't supposed to know where she goes."

"How did *you* find out?"

"I'm half-angel. I picked stuff up out of Deirdre's mind and did research on the darknet using your login."

"She's still associated with the Starks." Konig considered this as he absently stroked Nori's hair.

"Can you use that?" Nori asked.

"I might be able to," Konig said. "You've done good work, Nori. Thank you."

She blushed. "If you need anything else, you can tell me."

"I will," he said, sliding his hand briefly into her bodice again. "And I do." There was power in their kiss—lingering vestiges of that which he hadn't claimed during their hurried sexual interlude. It fed Konig, strengthening him in a way that even wine and ambrosia could not.

But when he stepped away, he realized he wasn't alone.

His mother was watching from among the veils. They fluttered in the motion of dancers on the other side, offering him only the barest glimpses of the Onyx Queen, and making her expression impossible to read.

How long had she been watching?

She drifted away.

"Damn," Konig muttered.

"What's wrong?" Nori hadn't seen Violet.

"Nothing, pet." He swatted her on the butt. "Get back to the party before anyone notices that you're missing. Stay away from the shifters. You don't want them to smell you."

Her cheeks turned pink, but she nodded.

She returned to the party.

Konig went looking for his mother.

"Where are you?" he muttered, pushing veils aside. Violet's perfume lingered on the air. It was the same scent she'd been wearing since he was a child who attended court cuddled in her lap.

The scent dissipated when he got to the hallway behind the equipment, and he didn't see his mother.

A different figure raced down the far end of the hall, vanishing around the corner.

Konig turned to fog—a pure energy form that only the strongest sidhe could assume. He slipped into the shadows unseen.

Leaving his body made it harder to see and hear. He got a vague sense of the person, more energy than anything else. It was probably human. Possibly female. Drenched in adrenaline. They didn't belong in that hallway.

An intruder.

By the time he regained his human form, the human had disappeared again.

Niflheimr was obscure to even a boy who'd grown up in the labyrinth of Myrkheimr. He opened nearby doors and peered down halls, but couldn't find the human.

Konig reached into his pocket to grip a white statuette. It was similar to the ones that Nori and Marion used to communicate. This one summoned Heather Cobweb to his side immediately, accompanied by one of the Raven Knights that Konig didn't recognize.

"Someone's in the palace who isn't attending the party. Someone dressed in a long black jacket, approximately this tall." Konig lifted his hand to his chest. "Detain them for me."

Heather pressed a fist to her chest and bowed.

She and the Raven Knight vanished.

FOURTEEN

Marion felt painfully conspicuous when she'd been dancing with Konig. They were the guests of honor who had dressed to make an impression. Even when she'd been enjoying herself with him, she'd only been able to think about the staring politicians.

When Seth took her onto the dance floor, she was probably far more conspicuous. She was with a man who wasn't on the guest list or dressed for the party. Or her fiancé, for that matter. But she didn't feel out of sorts. She was finally right where she was supposed to be.

"I thought you weren't going to come to my wedding," Marion said, shining a smile at him.

"This isn't your wedding," he pointed out. "It's just some party."

"And it's filled with the same people you don't

want to know about you," she said. "Aren't you worried one of the shifters will sniff you out?"

He bowed his head toward her ear. "Who'd think a god would dress like this?"

She giggled. "I don't care why you're here. I'm glad to see you."

His eyes went warm. "Yeah, I'm glad to see you too." He was so much shorter than Konig that they were nearly nose-to-nose when they danced like that. Seth was a lot less flashy in his dancing than Konig, too. It was a lot more like swaying in place. "Heck of a party."

"It's meant to be a way we can lobby for votes." She sighed. "It's bribery. Look at them." Marion nodded toward the couches along the wall.

Ruelle Myön had wasted no time getting what she wanted out of the party. The witch was currently being hand-fed dates by a naked sidhe draped across her chest.

On the couch beside them, a shifter Marion didn't recognize had wine poured into his mouth by a waiter.

And beyond that, there were movements among the shadowy pillars that Marion couldn't mistake for eating food.

"By the time the witching hour chimes, half these people will be involved in an orgy. It's the sidhe way," Marion said. "Orgasms for world peace."

Seth nearly choked. She giggled again.

"You're okay with this?" he asked when he regained the ability to speak.

Nobody had asked Marion that yet. They seemed to assume that becoming queen of an unseelie court meant that she'd want to live as the sidhe did. "No, I suppose I'm not. It's one thing for the sidhe to make love recreationally, so to speak. It's another to use it as a tool for coercion. Few mortals can resist sidhe magic, even if they want to."

"Sounds like there's not a lot of consent going around," Seth said, turning them in a slow circle. It gave Marion a great view of Ruelle and the sidhe who had disappeared up her skirt.

Her cheeks went hot. *Some engagement party.*

"I have a less coercive solution to gathering all the votes, if you're willing to entertain it," she said. "You won't like it."

"Hard to imagine something I'd like less than this," Seth said. He was looking at Marion with the kind of intensity that said he was trying not to see what Ruelle was up to.

"Appear in front of the council," Marion said. "Reveal yourself as the third god of the triad walking the Earth in mortal form. It should be easy to make them believe." She traced a finger over the glamour pendant nestled in the hollow of his throat. "Then tell them you endorse my wedding to Konig, and you want him to remain Prince of the Autumn Court."

She could tell by Seth's expression that she was right. He didn't like it.

"It would probably work," he admitted. "They're only voting because of what you said at the summit—how Elise and James don't want the angels in the Winter Court."

"Exactly. If one of the gods takes it back, then you'll also take the fear that Deirdre has instilled in them. Then I'll marry Konig, the peace treaty will encompass the Winter Court, and we'll be safe from further battling. Everyone, in theory, will be happy."

"Would it make *you* happy?" Seth asked. The magical twinkling starlight of the ballroom cast his strong features in deep shadows, but the scar on his bottom lip still glowed white.

"Yes," Marion said. It didn't sound at all convincing.

"If I come out like this...it'll change everything. I can't just say I'm the god of death without taking responsibility for it."

"There must be a way to continue caring for the Pit of Souls without betraying your nature."

Seth sighed. "Marion..."

"Please promise me that you'll think about it."

"I've already thought about becoming Death a lot. Here's the thing—being a demon-god isn't just a betrayal to my nature. It would destroy my future. It would destroy *me*."

Marion ran her thumb over the glamour pendant, feeling the crackle of energy under her skin. "You're eternal, Seth."

"My life isn't. I fought poverty, abuse, and a life as a werewolf hunter to become a doctor. Going to college was part of the reason I lost Rylie to Abel. And then I defied Elise and James to come back to life and save people, too." Seth's hand tightened on hers. "It'd be a hell of a sacrifice if I step into the role of Death and leave everything behind."

"It's okay," she said. "I know it was a terrible idea. I couldn't ever ask you to do something that huge."

"That's the thing," Seth said. "When you look at me like this, and you ask me to help you, it makes that sacrifice seem small."

Was the music even playing anymore? Marion couldn't seem to hear it over her pounding heart.

"I'll think about it," he said. "It's the only thing I can promise."

Marion swallowed hard. "That's not why you came to this party."

"No, I just came back from searching for Charity in Sheol." He shook himself like he was waking up from a dream. "Duat's guarded in a dome of balefire. I couldn't get in. It felt like she was there, though."

"Konig said he never saw her body. He just assumed she'd died."

"Doesn't matter. If she's locked in Duat by Arawn, we have to find a way to get her out." Seth spoke even quieter. "Can you come with me and help?"

Every fiber of Marion's being wanted to shout yes and race out of the ballroom with him at that moment. That was how she'd ended up in Sheol with him last time. That was why she'd almost died, and almost killed Seth too. And that was how she'd left the Winter Court vulnerable to Leliel's attack.

It was a selfish urge, and one that she couldn't entertain, no matter how tempting.

"I wish I could," Marion said softly.

"Your wedding isn't until tomorrow."

"I can't leave Niflheimr while it's full of guests. The wards would probably fail. And I must convince the council to vote for us. I'm sorry, Seth. I want to help Charity."

Seth sighed. "I know you do. I understand. I'd make the same choice in your position."

There was an unvoiced "but" following those words.

Marion waited for a moment to see if he'd finish his sentence, swaying in place with him as the music slowed. Even slow music performed by the denizens of the Autumn Court had a lot of rhythm to it, the kind of thing that made her want to roll her hips.

"What's your problem with the wedding?" Marion asked when Seth didn't elaborate. "I'm right, aren't I? You have a problem with the wedding. Don't tell me that you think I can't handle Niflheimr. I can. I don't need to be sidhe to rule."

"That's not it," Seth said. "Trust me, I know you. You were born to be a queen." He didn't give her enough time to preen over the compliment. "But we both know Konig's too smart to be mistaken about Charity's death. If he told you she died, he's lying."

The words gnawed a black hole in the pit of

her stomach. Such vulnerability and self-doubt hurt. "You've got no proof of that," Marion said, a little more sharply than she'd intended.

The kindness in Seth's eyes never faltered. "Well, and you shouldn't marry someone you're not in love with."

"I love him," Marion said. "I do."

"You deserve better than that. You deserve to be happy." They weren't whispering anymore, nor were they dancing, so they didn't need to be standing as close as they were.

"I'll be happy when I'm truly in charge of the Winter Court." Rylie wouldn't be able to sit Marion at the end of the table with the vampires during future council meetings. That was for certain.

"If you're sure." His callused hands were gentle on hers. "I hate to bring it up, but I still need the darknet servers. Now more than ever."

Cold reality jolted through her. "I can help with that." Marion glanced around the dance floor. Between the music, the buffet, and the wine, nobody was looking at them. Konig also had yet to return from whatever state business he had been addressing. They had a few minutes.

Marion was seized by a sense of adventure—a smaller one than that which had led her to follow Seth to Sheol, but adventure nonetheless. "Come with me." She caught Seth's hand and pulled him through fluttering veils behind the orchestra, cutting through the storage room to the hallway beyond.

Konig returned to the ballroom in time to see a flash of red as Marion vanished through the veils.

She wasn't alone.

Both Marion and her companion had vanished beyond the orchestra before Konig could tell whom she was with, though. The person didn't appear to be wearing a hooded sweater. It wasn't the intruder. Marion was likely just lobbying for votes, as a good queen-to-be should.

He grabbed a glass of cordial from a passing waiter. "Have you seen my mother?"

"That way," said the waiter, nodding toward the opposite side of the room. Few of the sidhe from the Autumn Court bothered with formalities where Konig was concerned. They'd all grown up and trained together. The only difference between Konig and the waiter was that Konig wasn't naked. "Something the matter?"

"There isn't enough wine," Konig said. "Open another cask."

"I'll see to it."

The prince sipped cordial as he weaved through the room, crossing to the pillars on the other side. He'd finished that cup and picked up a goblet of wine before finding her.

Violet was separate from the rest of the party, surrounded in a ring of Raven Knights who were combing an empty hallway. His mother was safe.

His momentary relief was overwhelmed by irritation when he realized that she was casting magic along the pillars.

"What do you think you're doing?" he asked in a low voice, stepping up behind his mother.

She didn't even glance his way. "What does it look like I'm doing, darling?"

"It looks like you're doing new wards, which will put you at the crux of the magic."

"Remarkable observation." Violet swept her hands like a conductor in front of an invisible orchestra. Light warped. "Maybe you won't waste my time asking inane questions in the future and instead employ your eyes and brain as you have just now."

He'd spent weeks trying to ignore that cloying tone she'd been using with him. Between the wine, the stress, and the adrenaline, he couldn't handle it anymore. "Is this meant to be punishment for what you saw me doing with Nori?"

Violet's hands stilled. "Actually, it's meant to save lives. Logan?" One of the Raven Knights walked over, carrying several stone spheres. "We found these affixed around the ballroom's perimeter. They're enchanted bombs. Don't worry —I've frozen them."

"Gods," Konig breathed, picking one up. It was heavy with magic. "How did these get into the world? The Knights checked all the guests."

"Your guess is as good as mine," Violet said.

Konig didn't really need to guess. "I just spied an intruder who isn't with any of the parties. I've sent Heather after him."

"That answers that." Violet waved Logan off, and he went back to removing the rest of the bombs.

"We should evacuate," Konig said.

"I think not. We've defused these. Let's not create a stir when we're already on such tenuous footing with the council." Violet shot a venomous look at her son. "Although I really shouldn't let you go through with the wedding at all. My counseling did nothing to instill respect for marriage."

So this was about Nori, in part. "Please. As if you care about whom I screw. I know what you're always up to during our parties."

"With your father's consent," she said. "I don't care what you do with your future wife's assistant or anyone else, whether they be servants, gentry, or demons. Even if you're engaged to someone who isn't sidhe, it doesn't change who we are or what we do. But you must do it with *consent*."

"Nori's very consenting," Konig said. "And I won't need her anymore after my wedding night with Marion."

Violet dropped her hands, but the magic remained thrashing around her. She turned chillingly empty eyes upon him. "At this point, you have a better chance of getting elected President of the North American Union than becoming King of the Winter Court."

Her words were well-targeted daggers into Konig's breast. Was that why she was casting wards on Niflheimr? Because she didn't see this as her son's home? "So smug," he growled.

"Smug about what? My son's failure to seize a kingdom? I'd take a lot more pride in being the mother of a success than I will in being right."

"And you wonder why I've fought to get out from under you for so long."

"I'll love you no matter how many ungrateful things you say to me. You'll still have a place in my court when your fiancée leaves you." She took Konig's hand. "A mother's love is inviolable."

He shook her off. "She'll never leave me."

"Where do you think she is now?" Violet asked. "Who is Marion hiding in shadowy corners with while you're tangled up with Nori?"

His fist clenched on the goblet's neck so suddenly that wine slopped over the side, wetting the wrist of his shirt.

He needed a refill.

Konig stalked away from his mother, and she went back to casting wards outside the ballroom.

She'd get more respectful once he became king.

If he became king.

Konig returned to the party. He was greeted warmly by the Oceania Witches, whom he knew on a social level. People he should have enjoyed talking with. He barely heard them.

Anger vibrated through his bones.

He caught sight of Deirdre Tombs alone near the buffet. She wasn't eating or drinking.

"Excuse me," he said, dismissing the Oceania

Witches.

Konig refilled his goblet and joined Deirdre.

She rolled a glowing blue cube of lethe between her forefinger and thumb. When he leaned against the wall beside her, she clutched it in her fist. "If you're going to be taking drugs, you may as well do it with the rest of the sidhe," Konig said. "Nobody will judge you here."

"I don't use anymore," Deirdre said, pocketing the lethe. "I like looking at it. The pretty colors help me think."

"What a waste of good lethe." The wine was hot in his veins, emboldening him. If his mother didn't believe he could take over the Winter Court, then the surest way to prove her wrong would be to confront the problem head-on. "Let's talk somewhere alone."

"I'm not going anywhere with you."

"You don't want anyone else to hear what I have to say," Konig said. He gestured at the dancers just a few feet away with his goblet. "Wouldn't it be terrible if all these people learned the truth about you?"

Deirdre's eyes darkened. "You don't have the stones to bully me."

At that moment, Konig felt like he had the "stones" for anything. All the rage that he couldn't take out on his mother was clawing at the inside of his throat. "I know you're connected to the Stark terrorists," Konig said in a low voice. "I know you're spending months at a time on their property in Africa. If you don't want everyone else to know that, you'll cancel the vote."

Deirdre folded her arms. "Oh yeah? Is that what you know?"

"Cancel the vote," he said more firmly.

Her flesh shimmered with faint flames. It lifted her hair around her shoulders as though a breeze blew in her face. "Or else what? You think I'm afraid of you telling people I like to vacation in Jo'burg?"

"I could have old investigations into you reopened."

"I doubt that. I seriously do." Deirdre leaned on the buffet table, which had been grown out of ice. She was hot enough that the surface began to sweat. "You've got no idea what you're talking about, pretty boy, and there's *nothing* you can do to me. But there's a lot I can do to you if you piss me off."

"I'm not afraid of you."

"That's not what it looks like. You wouldn't be in my face if you weren't." Deirdre sniffed him, and she recoiled, nose wrinkling. "And you really wouldn't need liquid courage to do it if you weren't afraid."

"The Secretary of the Office of Preternatural Affairs is here," Konig said. "I'll tell him everything right now."

"He already knows. Surprised? You wouldn't be if you'd done real research."

The melting table dripped cold onto Konig's shoe. He twitched.

Deirdre smiled. "I joined the terrorists because

I was undercover for the OPA. We moved Stark's family to South Africa under protective custody, and I check in on them all the time. Have you met the Alpha, Rylie Gresham? You know what a soft spot she's got for family bullshit? And you know how kindly she'd react to you threatening this family I'm taking care of?"

Konig didn't know. He knew very little about that, in fact. Rylie was a matter that Marion handled.

Deirdre flared until he could feel the sheer heat radiating from her shifter-flesh.

"Right now, Rylie's the only ally you've got for this wedding because of that soft spot of hers, but it'll vanish if you flap your mouth," she said softly. "And for what? I can't even cancel the vote. It's locked in."

He was getting hot now too, but not from her fire—from frustration.

Konig should have gotten more information from Nori. Shouldn't have jumped the gun. Should have waited.

"I've been reading up on you, too, Prince ErlKonig," Deirdre said. "I know you've got this election rigged."

He took care not to show his surprise. "You don't know anything."

"You're hours from having the wards on Niflheimr fail completely because a non-sidhe steward's been in control for so long. If you don't take control, then the whole Winter Court's going to be exposed—and the steward will have to surrender control of Niflheimr to your parents. They couldn't even set foot in the palace until recently. So either way, the Autumn Court's going to end up in charge." She leaned in close, glowering at him. "I'll have an army ready for when your parents move their angel allies into this plane."

Konig emptied his cup and slammed it on the table, splashing water over the side. "That's not true. My parents never took Niflheimr because they didn't want it."

"They wanted it all right," Deirdre said. "They even gave aid to the Summer Court's invading forces back in the day. But the Winter Queen had them locked out until Marion took over. Now all they have to do is wait."

That wasn't what his parents had told him.

"They were friends with the Winter Queen and King," he protested. "You're lying."

"Bet I know more about sidhe history than you do. I get around more than your average shifter." She shoved the cube of lethe into his hand. "Take this and enjoy a few numb hours. We all know this is going to end in war before the week's out."

FIFTEEN

The music from the ballroom was much quieter with a couple walls of ice in the way. It faded quickly as Marion took Seth toward the bedrooms. The temperature also rapidly dropped. By the time they got to the staircase, she was shivering. "Why's it more urgent to get into the servers now?" Marion asked, teeth chattering.

Seth jogged to keep up with her. "Lucifer says there's information about the location of a mysterious weapon on there. And I don't know if you noticed, but there's a lot of people in your palace right now who shouldn't have mysterious weapons."

"What kind of weapon?"

"The mysterious kind. That's seriously all I know. He thinks everyone's after the servers so that they can find it in this other dimension, this missing ethereal plane."

"Could the weapon be balefire?" Marion asked. "It must come from somewhere strange, since pure balefire burns through everything."

"I hadn't thought of that." Seth grabbed her elbow. "If there's information on balefire on the darknet, we could get into Duat." Which meant they would be able to save Charity.

"Then let's hope you have more success finding the darknet servers than I have." Marion stopped in front of a towering bedroom door carved with the image of elaborate circuitry. She unlocked the handle with a wave of her hand. The cogs along the hinges clicked and thumped, whirring into motion so that the doors could swing open. "This is where the Hardwicks lived in the Winter Court. They started the darknet. One of the refugees suggested I might be able to get server access through here, but I already searched these rooms once and didn't find anything."

The Hardwicks had been rich in taste, and much less blue-collar than the king, who had decorated Niflheimr in icy cogs and chains. Their furniture was high-end Danish stuff. It must have been difficult to import to the Middle Worlds. There was a reason that the sidhe mostly grew their furniture using magic.

Seth shut and locked the door behind them before starting to search.

"I believe there are secret passages throughout Niflheimr," Marion said, scuffing her feet along the tiled floors and listening for hollow parts. It was hard to tell with all the ice. "One of the other refugees, Ymir—he's been sneaking around somehow."

Seth started feeling along the bookshelves. "Makes sense. It's not a good castle without secret passages."

Marion watched him methodically investigate the sitting room, the dining room, and the attached kitchen. She hugged herself, trying to rub warmth into her upper arms. "Does this mean you've decided to become a vampire?"

"Probably," Seth said without looking back. "Did I ever tell you I tried to become a werewolf once?"

Marion's heart flipped. "So you could mate with Rylie?"

"Yeah, but it turned out I was immune to the curse. Vampire's not that much worse than werewolf, and miles better than being a god whose job is to kill people."

"Rylie wants to kill me." The words leaped out unbidden.

Seth turned from inspecting the underside of a lamp. "What? No she doesn't."

"When I was looking up information on the OPA databases, I looked into my file as well. Rylie recorded testimony saying that I'm dangerous. She believes that it's important to have plans in place to kill me."

To his credit, he didn't try to deny it again. He raked a hand over his hair. "Jesus, Rylie."

"Just think," Marion said, trying to make her

tone light, "in another universe where you mated to Rylie, you'd probably be planning to kill me, too."

Seth set the lamp down. "Listen, Marion. There's no universe in which I'd try to kill you. Not if I was a werewolf, not when I'm a death god, not even if I was possessed by a demon. *None*." He took her by the elbows, and his brow furrowed. "Damn, you're cold."

"Sleeveless dress." Her chin quivered. "Doesn't look good for the future Queen of the Winter Court to be freezing in her own palace, does it?"

"Nobody's going to judge you while we're sneaking around in condemned parts of your palace." He slipped the jacket off of his shoulders and settled it over Marion.

The right pocket weighed heavily against her side. She slipped her hand in. "What's this?"

"A wedding present," Seth said. "I almost forgot."

She pulled it out.

It was a water bottle with the label ripped off.

"Oh my," Marion said. "You know, when you do a gift registry, you always realize that you must have forgotten a few things, but water bottles... I suppose that *is* the gift you get the mage who already has everything."

He didn't smile back. "That's from Mnemosyne. The river of memory in Sheol."

It suddenly felt much heavier in Marion's hands. "Oh."

"I don't know if it'll work. Everything was

supposed to be in the Canope. But I thought, if there's a chance..." He shrugged.

Marion returned the bottle to the pocket. "Thank you, Seth. I'm not going to drink it. But thank you."

His eyebrows lifted. "Why?"

"I've spent weeks coming to terms with the fact that the woman I used to be is gone. Dead, in a way. But nothing was lost when the Canope broke. I truly believe that."

"Hey." Seth's tone was sharper than a knife. "Don't talk about yourself like that."

"Very well. I won't say it out loud where you can hear me."

He shoved her shoulder, gently. "Be nice to yourself. Out loud and in your head. I've got enough self-loathing for you, me, and everyone else in the Winter Court."

Marion's heart unknotted and turned inside out and back-flipped. "*You* have self-loathing?"

"I drank Mnemosyne," Seth said. "I wanted to know what kind of god stuff I'd forgotten becoming avatar. And now I know why I came back."

She didn't need to drink any water out of the Nether Worlds to know that. "To save Rylie from Deirdre."

"That's the thing, Marion. I didn't come back to save Rylie. I saw her die and...I didn't do anything. I didn't *care*."

She ran her fingers over his knuckles, as though soothing a hurt from knocking a door too hard. "How do you know that you didn't let her die because that's the natural order of things?"

"Rylie's death isn't natural. She gets shot."

"All death is as natural as being born. It's something that happens to all of us eventually. We don't get to choose." The words weren't touching Seth. Marion could see the hurt in him, and she wanted to take it away, but she couldn't. "I wouldn't be happy with that answer either, just so you know. Nothing is beyond my control. If I were a god, I'd want to save everyone too, just like you."

That elicited a small smile from him. "I didn't want to save anyone. I didn't care about anything." Seth's eyes had gone unfocused, seeing to places and times that Marion couldn't imagine. "Being God is the ultimate detachment. The universe moves through you, but you don't have anything to do with it."

"Something inspired you to become an avatar."

"A grudge against Elise," he said.

"You willed yourself back immediately after Genesis. I'm sure it was for a better reason than annoying my sister."

"Coincidence."

"You won't let me talk about myself badly, but you're dismissing your own strengths as though they're nothing." Marion smoothed her fingers over the back of his hand again. "You are anything but an unfeeling god, Dr. Flynn."

He finally focused on her. It was the old pseudonym that had snapped him out of himself.

"When I become a god again, I'm not going to care about you either. I won't care that you're marrying Konig. And I won't care that you'll die."

Each statement lashed out at her, though she knew that it was part of Seth's self-flagellation, whipping himself with something he considered bitter truth. "I may not be a god, but I know if I walked outside of time, I would never stop caring." Her throat worked. It felt like she was swallowing needles. "I wouldn't stop caring about *you*."

Seth's only response was to pull her against his chest.

The embrace surprised her, though not unpleasantly. She let her arms creep around him carefully to tighten her fingers on the small of his back, where the fatal wounds from the Hounds had yet to spread.

The locks on the hallway door clicked. The handles shifted.

Marion turned, lifting her hands reflexively to cast spells.

Who would be trying to enter the bedroom of a sidhe couple who hadn't lived in Niflheimr for years?

"Pantry," Seth whispered.

He dragged her away before she could summon any spells to mind.

"This is my palace! I don't need to hide!" Marion hissed back.

"Don't you want to know who else is looking for the darknet?" Seth pushed her through the door beside the fire pit, slipping in behind her. He left it open an inch so that he could watch the room on the other side.

There wasn't a lot of space in the pantry for two people and one voluminous party dress. Unexpected adrenaline thrilled through Marion at the dig of the shelf into her spine and the press of Seth's knee against hers. They weren't as close as they had been while dancing, but it was much quieter and more private, and her pounding heart was too aware of it.

Seth's hand crept to the small of his back as he peered through the crack in the door. He wasn't distracted by Marion. He was focused on what was going on, instead of how much warmer it was to be closed up in a tiny pantry with someone who wasn't her fiancé.

She wasn't shivering anymore.

Marion lifted onto her toes to look over Seth's shoulder.

Whoever entered the Hardwicks' room wasn't dressed for the party. It was a short, broad figure cloaked in a hooded sweater, like the kind purchased in university bookstores. Not the kind that a person would wear to a fancy political gala.

The person was walking briskly towards the pantry.

"Seth," Marion hissed.

He pushed her back with one hand, while the other crept to the small of his back to draw a handgun.

When she took a step closer to the rear corner of the pantry, her heel slipped on uneven floor.

Marion fell with a tiny gasp.

Her hand flew out. Her reaction time was good enough that she realized she shouldn't grab the pantry shelves—not unless she wanted to pull a lot of jarred fruit on top of her head—but not good enough to remain standing without help. So her fingers closed on the back of Seth's shirt.

Both of them hit the ground with a loud *thump*. Probably too loud to hope that the intruder didn't hear it.

Seth was braced above Marion on his elbows. It was too dark in the pantry to see his face clearly —and dark enough that light glimmered through his shirt where he'd been wounded, despite the glamour hanging from his neck.

"Are you okay?" Seth sounded alarmed, like he couldn't imagine what could have made her fall.

She couldn't seem to draw in a chestful of air. It had nothing to do with Seth atop her or the snugness of her dress.

Her fingers spread across his chest. The energy underneath called to her, begging to be unleashed. But above that energy, there was nothing but human muscle and flesh.

"No," Marion said. "I'm not okay."

The pantry door flew open. The intruder in the hoodie stood on the other side.

Seth was on his knees instantly, turning to bring the gun to bear.

His reaction wasn't as fast as that of the sidhe.

Heather Cobweb and a Raven Knight materialized behind the intruder in a flash of light.

The relief that Marion felt was only secondary to the shock—not just from suddenly finding herself in an apartment filled with sidhe, but being seen by Konig's guard with Seth.

"On the ground!" Heather commanded, her belt knife drawn.

The intruder didn't argue, but they also weren't in a hurry to comply. Marion thought she heard curse words grumbled as the hooded figure got down.

Heather ripped the hood off to expose the intruder.

Dana McIntyre rolled her eyes. "I take it I'm under arrest?"

Dana was clearly a woman accustomed to being arrested. She made herself comfortable in the dungeon, propping her feet up on the wall and reclining against the floor. The sidhe's magical bindings didn't cramp her style at all.

She also wasn't intimidated by the company she kept. The Raven Knights and Heather Cobweb were bad enough on their own. Having the Onyx Queen, Seth, Marion, and Konig looming over her should have made her slightly nervous. Add in the fact that Jibril was waiting in the hall...

Yet Dana was as relaxed as though she were having a spa day.

"Really, Dana?" Marion asked, arms folded

over her chest. "Are you so angry at me that you'd invade my wedding festivities? I know I hurt you, but this—this is *low*."

"Self-centered as always. You think everything's a personal grudge against you," Dana said.

"I'm confused," Heather said. "Who is this, exactly?"

"Dana McIntyre is a triadist and mercenary who operates out of Las Vegas." Marion sighed. "And she's my sister."

That surprised a laugh out of Heather. "*She's* your sister?"

"Not by blood," Marion muttered. She shot a look at Konig to encourage him to back her up. The Knights had retrieved him from the party after apprehending Dana, and he still had a full goblet of wine. His eyes were a little glazed from excessive drink.

"I don't do much mercenary work. Call me a spellsword," Dana said.

"At the moment we're calling you a potential assassin," Konig snarled. "You don't want to be a potential assassin. The sidhe don't like those types of people. Right, Heather?"

The archer responded by passing her belt knife from her left hand to her right. She smiled faintly.

"You're stupid and I don't like you," Dana said.

Konig's face darkened. "You—"

"She didn't go for the party because she wasn't trying to kill anyone," Marion said. "I have to wonder how you got in, though. You're not on the guest list—although you could have been if you'd asked nicely."

"Then I'd have had to go dance," Dana said. "I don't dance." She shrugged a shoulder. "Your wards are going bad. I got in the same way I get in anywhere."

"You're not a planeswalker," Marion said.

Dana shrugged again. She wasn't offering information she didn't need to.

It was easy to imagine what Dana did, though. Even though she didn't use magic herself, she had dozens of enchanted weapons. It stood to reason that not all her artifacts were offensive.

"If you weren't planning to assassinate anyone, then what are these for?" asked the Onyx Queen, gesturing to the Raven Knights.

One of them stepped forward. He was cradling grenade-sized spheres in his hands, which sparked with crimson energy. They didn't just resemble grenades—they *were* grenades, meant to explode with magic rather than gunpowder.

"We found those placed around the ballroom," Konig explained at Marion's expression of surprise.

She turned on her sister. "Oh, Dana. *Why?*"

Dana snorted. "Arawn's gathering energy by killing people and burning their spirits in balefire. He needs a few hundred souls more in order to ascend to Earth. Where do you think he wants to get those from?"

"Our wedding," Konig said. "He wants to

harvest his dead from our wedding."

"Exactly," Dana said. "I thought I'd blow a few charges to scare you guys into canceling it. And I figured I'd find the darknet servers while you were distracted."

Konig flung his free hand into the air. "Those stupid servers again. Everyone's on about those servers!"

"Why do *you* want them?" Marion asked. "Is it about the weapon?"

Dana paled. Her thoughts fizzed across the surface of her mind, more transparent than Marion had ever seen before. She hadn't thought Marion knew about that.

"What is the weapon?" Seth asked. "Do you know?"

"Doesn't matter." Dana folded her arms obstinately. "Arawn wants it. Leliel wants it. Everyone wants it. I'm doing y'all a favor by trying to get there first."

And Dana had thought that setting off a few bombs would fix everything. It was spectacularly bad planning, yet it seemed so very...Dana. She was a punch to the face in human form.

Marion certainly felt as though she'd been punched. She had one hell of a headache developing. "You could have just told me about this when I was in Las Vegas."

"I wanted to beat Arawn without having to deal with you," Dana said.

"I don't see why Arawn's plans are your problem anyway."

"Because if he ascends, he'll probably destroy the Pit of Souls on his way up. And then what happens? I dunno. It won't be good." Dana sat up straighter. "Cancel the wedding. You've got to shut down Niflheimr completely."

Konig laughed and drained his goblet of wine. "The wedding goes on as planned. We won't be cowed by petty threats." Clearly he meant Dana, not Arawn.

"Why don't we move the wedding to Myrkheimr?" Violet suggested.

Marion would have rather swallowed needles than have the wedding in the home of her overbearing mother-in-law. "I can't leave Niflheimr. The wards could fail completely if I leave again."

"But there's sun in the Autumn Court," Seth said, rubbing his chin thoughtfully. "Arawn can't go in the sun, and neither can people that he possesses with his demons. Then there won't be wedding guests in Niflheimr, either."

Dana glared black hatred at him. "Yeah, that's the obvious solution to this, isn't it? Move the wedding's location. That will fix everything."

"It's less vulnerable than the Winter Court on multiple levels," Violet said, as if the decision had been made. She waved to Heather Cobweb. "See to it that everything begins relocating immediately."

The archer bowed and exited.

Through the swinging door, Marion glimpsed Jibril watching. He would surely be hearing everything.

"There's another option to protect Niflheimr," Dana said. "Marion could just ask the gods to take care of it."

She was looking at Seth when she said that.

Marion tried to catch her eye, shaking her head.

No, Dana. Please don't.

"The gods haven't shown any sign of being directly involved in affairs to this point," Violet said. "I don't see why that would change now."

Dana looked directly at Marion, saw that she was shaking her head, and grinned. Dana's teeth were uneven. The canines were yellow. "It'll change now," Dana said, "because the third god of the triad is standing among us right now. Seth Wilder is a god."

SIXTEEN

Until the moment that Dana spoke, Seth had been ignored by everyone in the room—the Raven Knights, the royalty, even Marion.

Seth Wilder is a god.

And he was suddenly the most interesting person there.

Marion turned to him with an apology on her lips, but he didn't hear it.

Grief, anger, and disbelief were etched on the faces of every sidhe in the room. Seth didn't need them to share their stories of Genesis to imagine what they were all so upset about. He'd heard enough stories while working at Mercy Hospital: families lost under collapsing buildings, husbands eaten by demons, children who never came back after the void consumed them.

As soon as Dana named him as a god, all of

that grief was turned toward him.

Marion reached for Seth.

He left before they could touch.

When Seth snapped his fingers, he didn't have a location in mind. He just wanted to be *away*, and he was.

He appeared in a bedroom elsewhere in the Winter Court. He was standing beside an unremarkable bed with about a thousand pillows piled against the headboard, and adjacent to an open closet with skirt suits hanging from the hook inside.

It wasn't Marion's bedroom or the one where the Hardwicks had lived, so it took him a moment to realize what had drawn him there, of all the places in the universe he could have gone.

Those nude-colored skirt suits were the kind of thing Rylie was wearing these days.

Once he recognized her clothes, he heard the murmur of her voice on the other side of the wall and felt the call of life and death that he associated with the werewolf Alpha.

He nudged the bedroom door open with a knuckle but hung back where he wouldn't be seen.

In the sitting room, a dozen people sat around a long table, all of them still dressed for the gala in fancy dresses and tuxedoes. Rylie was at the nearest end, sharing tea and appetizers in the form of dainty meat cubes. Raw meat meant shifters. Seth was shocked to see that one of those shifters was Deirdre Tombs.

Seth momentarily contemplated taking Deirdre down right at that instant before anyone could react.

Rylie was facing away from him, but her head lifted, tipped to the side. Her nostrils flared.

She smelled him.

"Excuse me," Rylie said to the others at the table. "I forgot that I'm meant to have another meeting in my rooms in a few minutes. Would you mind...?"

"Not at all." Deirdre Tombs stood up, and half the table stood with her. All of them must have come with the American Gaean Commission. It was arrogant—maybe even naïve—for Rylie to have allowed so many members of an opposing faction into her private rooms.

His memory of Deirdre standing over Rylie, gun still smoking from the shot that had killed her, was far too vivid.

Deirdre's people left, and then Rylie murmured a few words to her personal guard, and they were gone too.

Only then did she turn to smile at the corner in which he lurked.

"Hey," Rylie said softly. Seth emerged from the bedroom. He was wearing the glamour, but her gaze shifted down to his shirt, as though expecting to see the gaping maw of his ribcage again. "This is a pleasant surprise. I hope it's a social call."

"It's not," Seth said.

She unbuttoned her suit jacket, slid it down her shoulders, and folded it over the back of a chair. "Then what do you need?"

"I don't really know," he admitted. "I had to get away and didn't think too much about where I was going. Dana McIntyre told everyone what I am. They *know*."

"Dana's here?" Rylie asked. "Color me shocked. I didn't realize Marion and Dana were still on speaking terms."

"They're not. Dana tried to blow up the engagement party."

Rylie's hands flew to cover her mouth. "Oh no. And then she told everyone?"

"The Autumn Queen and half a dozen Raven Knights," Seth said. "It'll get out fast. Everyone's going to know soon." Each word made him feel heavier as the reality of it sank in.

His identity had been revealed in Niflheimr at a time when word could spread the fastest. The most powerful preternaturals were in attendance with all their aides.

Seth dropped onto Rylie's couch, cradling his head in his hands.

"What am I going to do?" he asked. "I don't want to be a god."

"We don't get to choose leadership, Seth. It chooses us." Rylie would know best. She had never asked to be Alpha, but she had risen in power until she became capable of controlling other werewolves. He had seen how it changed her over the years that had followed.

"It's not leadership that chose me. It was Elise. This is her fault."

"Does it matter where blame belongs?"

"Yes," Seth said. "Because all this bullshit—the whole world dying and changing, and the war between gods—that was Elise's fault. She put me in front of it. And when Dana told people what I was, they looked at me like Genesis was *my* fault."

Rylie sat next to him, carrying a cup of tea and a saucer. "Just because it's hard doesn't mean it's not worth doing. I don't have experience being a god, but the shifters see me like a queen, and... well, I can tell you that leadership sucks. You have to be a face for everyone to direct adulation and anger toward. Elise would be terrible at it. You're not. You're made for this, Seth."

"I'm not," Seth said. "I'm really not. I can handle rounds at an emergency room, but that's worlds different from being responsible for *everything*."

"You also ran my pack for ages." She smiled weakly. "I struggled after Genesis without you."

He frowned. "When I visited, you said everything was fine."

"Yeah, I told you everything was fine," Rylie said. "But it wasn't. God, it wasn't fine, Seth, *nothing* was fine."

She might as well have punched him, it hurt so much. "Why didn't you tell me that? I'd have stayed to help."

"You had always wanted to become a doctor, and you were doing it. You were finally living the life you always wanted before I ruined it." She took a long, slow drink of her tea, shoulders trembling as though she was trying to hold back tears. "I wasn't going to ruin it for you again."

"Elise took care of the ruining for us this time," Seth said.

"She knows what she's doing. As a god, you'll be able to save countless people, just like you always wanted."

It wasn't just like he wanted. Not even a little bit. "I'm supposed to be the god who kills everyone. Even you." Seth glanced at her, and he couldn't shut out the vision of her death. Not this time. "When you die, Rylie—"

She lifted her hands to stop him. "Please don't."

"Deirdre Tombs kills you. Arrest her, have Abel murder her, whatever. You've got to stop her before she can do it."

Rylie heaved a sigh. "Oh, Seth. I told you I don't want to know."

"But now you do," he said, a little too fiercely. "You have to do something about it."

"Deirdre Tombs is a good woman." She set her teacup down. "A good woman, but I'm not at all surprised she kills me. If it's going to be anyone... well, at least it's her."

He stared at her in shock. "You're happy about that?"

"Deirdre does nothing without good reason. If she kills me, I trust that it needs to happen." She took Seth's hands, her fingers still as soft as he remembered them, her eyes as gentle. "You need to trust it, too."

"You're not at all shaken by this."

"I'll need time to think about it." She raked her bottom lip between her teeth. "God, I wish you hadn't told me."

Rylie stood up and paced away from him.

Seth felt numb inside.

He shouldn't have told her.

But he had, because he selfishly wanted her to do something about it. He thought she'd fix it.

Instead, she was going to let it haunt her.

"I'm sorry," Seth said.

"Leadership sucks," Rylie whispered, so quiet that he was compelled to cross the icy room to stand beside her. "We make sacrifices. We change."

"You haven't changed that much. You're still as beautiful to me as the day we met at summer camp."

A flicker of a smile crossed her lips. "You haven't changed much, either. You're still sweet. When we were at the sanctuary together..." Rylie swallowed hard and reached up to cup Seth's cheek. "Even before you left, I hadn't seen you look happy like that in years."

He put his hand over hers. "I've missed you."

"It's not me you're looking at when you're happy," Rylie said.

"I don't..." His mouth was too dry to finish the sentence. He swallowed hard. "She's getting married to someone else."

Rylie sagged. "Okay. Wow."

"I'm just saying that nothing's happening

there," Seth said. "I like her a lot, but...nothing's happening."

"Maybe it should. You have to let me go, Seth. You should have let me go years ago."

"Yeah, like how you let me go and married Abel."

She grimaced. "That's different."

"And this isn't about you," Seth said with more conviction. "Marion's getting married and she's Elise's sister. And..."

And he had promised he'd love Rylie forever.

Failing that, he'd promised to be alone.

He walked away from Rylie, seeking somewhere he could breathe a little more easily. There was no air left in the room. His heart was laboring to beat.

Rylie touched his elbow. "It's okay, Seth. If you have feelings for Marion, it's not your fault. It might not even be a coincidence. After all...God works in mysterious ways."

It didn't take long to move the wedding. With all of the Raven Knights employing the full force of sidhe magic, they transplanted decorations, guests, and their belongings while it was still nighttime in the Autumn Court.

Marion didn't feel safer in Myrkheimr than Niflheimr, even though the wards in the Autumn Court were much stronger, and the grounds were teeming with more security than merely the Raven Knights. Every one of the council invitees to Marion's wedding had moved to the Middle Worlds, taking their entourages with them. So much security patrolled the gardens that it was safer than magical Fort Knox.

If they'd had the engagement party in the Autumn Court, then yes, those protections would have stood up against Dana. Marion just wasn't confident they'd have the same effect against Arawn.

At least she'd started to turn her Niflheimr bedroom into something that felt homey. Her room in Myrkheimr still felt uncomfortably alien to her, even if the breeze was much warmer and the closet was filled with clothing in her size.

"It's almost over," she murmured, gazing out at the gardens as sidhe swept through, draping cloths from tree branches and shooting pixie lights among the leaves.

They'd be having the reception among the fountains of honey after the wedding. The wedding that was now only sixteen hours away.

Marion had nothing left to do that night, but she felt too sick to sleep.

She turned to go to bed anyway. A figure stood in the doorway.

Her heart leaped into her throat at the sight of the tall, willowy figure. She'd had an assassin enter her bedroom through the balcony before, and his silhouette had looked very much like that one, framed by the fluttering curtains.

This time, when he stepped forward, it was not a nameless killer, but Konig.

"Hey," she started to say, but the other words vanished from her mind when she saw his expression.

Konig looked angry.

"My mother saw you," he said.

Even at that distance, she could smell the wine on him.

"Excuse me?"

"You and Seth," he said. "My mother saw you sneaking off with him at our engagement party. Heather found you in a closet with him."

"We were searching the Hardwicks' room for secret passages. That's all."

"So it's true. Violet told me that she saw you running around with someone, but I thought she was lying until I saw you in the dungeon with... him." He looked so *angry*. An empty wine goblet hung from one hand.

She edged around him into her bedroom. "You were busy or else I would have told you."

"Sure you would have. Sure." He took a step for each of hers, sliding along the opposite wall. He didn't just smell like alcohol. He looked like a man who'd been beaten down and crushed under heel. "My mother's always been overbearing, but she loves me. That might be the problem, I think. She wants the best for me." He stopped in front of her cabinet, opening it to find a bottle of wine Marion hadn't known she had. He surveyed the label. "Good year. Want a glass?"

"I don't think this is the time to drink," Marion said.

He slammed the point of the bottle opener into the cork so hard that she couldn't help jumping.

Konig filled his cup, drained it, and filled it again.

"You're not overbearing," he said. "You're independent. That's what I've always admired about you. You don't *need* me. A free agent! How fucking *nice* that is, after so many years choking under my royal parents' fists."

Another long drink.

"This is quite the mood," Marion said lightly. "Did you have trouble with your business at the engagement party?"

"Trouble? Other than being openly defied by Deirdre Tombs, finding your stupid sister trying to blow up my ballroom, and learning that you're screwing a god? What kind of trouble would there be?"

She couldn't talk to him when he was being like that. There was no point. She braced herself and said, "I think you've had enough wine now. Why don't you crawl into bed?"

"Alone?" He barked a laugh. "Why bother? Do you get off on seeing me suffer?"

He hurled the goblet to the floor with a loud clang. Marion leaped back.

"My mother is overbearing, but she loves me," he said. "You're not overbearing. And I think you don't love me."

"You know that isn't true," she said.

"Then why the fuck did Heather see Seth on top of you? That's why it's so easy for you to hold out on me. You're getting plenty of dick on the side."

The blood drained from her face. "I'm not. I would never."

"Don't lie to me," Konig said. "Heather saw you."

"She didn't see what you think," she said.

The last word was barely out of her mouth before he swung.

The next thing she knew, Marion was on the floor, dazed, fingertips brushing a hot bruise on her cheekbone.

He had backhanded her.

The man she was about to marry...he had struck her.

Confusion and denial were too strong to leave room for anything else. Certainly there was no room for thoughts about self-defense, because the idea she'd have to defend herself against Konig at all was insane.

Her friend, her ally, her lover—someone she was utterly safe with.

He'd hurt her.

Konig seemed to realize he'd crossed a line. All the fury that had drenched him in earlier moments was replaced by shock.

"Marion," he said, dropping beside her.

She flinched away. "Don't."

His cold fingers brushed along her wounded cheek. "You see what you do to me? You see how much I need you, and how it hurts me when you do this?"

"Hurts *you*?" She was the one who'd gotten slapped.

"If you hadn't been so gods-damned intimate with Seth—and if you weren't holding out on me..." His hands tightened on her shoulders. "I love you too much, princess. You can't treat me like this after everything I've done for you. I'm risking my life for you. My title. *Everything*."

For all that she should have feared him, the heartache in his words only made her want to cling to him. Hurt and comfort, all encapsulated in one man.

Marion wrapped her arms around his ribcage, tucking her head under his chin. "I'm sorry."

"You're sorry? You're *sorry*? You should be a hell of a lot more than sorry, princess. It's your selfishness that left Niflheimr open to Leliel's attack in the first place. Now your selfishness is going to make us lose the vote. Don't be *sorry*. Be better!" Konig shoved her off of him. In his absence, she was colder on the inside than the Winter Court.

"I'm trying to do better. I am."

"I'm afraid your best just might not be good enough."

She stood on wavering legs. She'd fallen more from shock than because he'd hit her too hard, but she still felt the ripples of the impact through her entire body. "What more could I do, Konig? You keep talking about what you've given up, but what about me?"

He laughed. "Dana was right. It's always about you."

"I'm giving up my life for this! I wouldn't have even agreed to marry you after all you've done if I weren't!"

Konig stopped moving.

He turned slowly, and his look was as hard as another slap.

"Amazing," he said. "Your best will never be good enough for the world, and it seems like my love will never be good enough for you, either."

"Konig—"

"Are you in love with Seth?" he interrupted.

"No," she said reflexively, without thinking about it. If there was anything she knew at this point, it was that confessing complicated feelings for anyone but Konig would do nothing but get her into trouble.

"So you've been sneaking around with him because you're a slut."

Her eyes widened. "No! Gods, Konig, I didn't even think words like that were part of a sidhe's vocabulary. You have orgies rather than shaking hands with people to say hello. Slut? I mean, *really*."

"But you're no sidhe. Sometimes I doubt you're an angel." His hand came out of his pocket. He was holding a golden cuff—the truth bracelet that Marion had made for the summit. "Are you in love with Seth? Are you lying to me?"

She stepped backwards. "I told you already."

"How am I supposed to trust you?"

Konig flashed forward, using the power of the sidhe to leap within their worlds to slam into her. Her back struck the wall.

She slipped. Fell to the floor.

He pinned her down with his weight, fingers shackling her arm. He shoved the bracelet over Marion's hand. The magic sank into her immediately.

"Are you in love with him, or are you just some whore?" It was horrifying to hear those words coming from Konig's face—his perfect, princely sidhe face, which Marion had so often gazed at adoringly. But while he spoke venom, he looked broken. Vulnerable. Afraid.

She wouldn't have responded if she'd had any choice.

"I love him," Marion said, unable to help it. "He's my friend, Konig. More than my friend. He's my God."

The silence weighed heavily on them.

He pushed back to sit on his knees, leaving her pinned underneath him even though he no longer held her arms. Marion ripped off the bracelet and tossed it across the room. It vanished underneath her couch.

Konig got up.

Marion did, too.

They stared at each other from opposite sides of the couch.

"You're lucky I'm still willing to even try to marry you after this," Konig finally said softly.

"I've always known you were selfish, but I never realized how cruel you could be."

He turned to leave.

She watched him going with sickness gnawing at her gut—a desperate need to fix things, to make him forgive her.

"Please wait," she said.

"Don't speak to me!" Konig roared with shocking, overwhelming fury, spinning on her again. He flung a hand out as his magic exploded.

They were too distant for him to strike her physically again. But unseelie energy knew no limits in the Autumn Court. It connected with her flesh even as it electrified her innards, hurling her off of her feet so that she smashed into the bookshelf beside her balcony door.

Marion fell in a rain of books and trinkets and burning tears.

She knew nothing but pain.

When the pain subsided enough for her to lift her head, Konig was gone.

SEVENTEEN

By the time Seth left Rylie's bedroom, the other wedding parties had relocated to the Autumn Court. Only a few Raven Knights remained to guard the palace, and in Marion's absence, the wards were weak enough that Seth could go anywhere he wanted.

The Onyx Queen's wedding decorations were also wearing down quickly. The Winter Court wanted to revert to its barren nature, untainted by the magic of the Autumn Court, and everything green had already been encased in ice. It wouldn't be long before it was gone entirely, absorbed by the glassy walls or torn down by harsh wind.

Seth didn't come across a single living soul on his way into the depths of Niflheimr, though he knew there should have been some around. A few refugees Marion had managed to save; a handful of Raven Knights.

And Dana McIntyre, far below ground.

It was trivial to phase himself beyond the sidhe guarding her. Nobody saw him going into the cell where Dana McIntyre was being kept.

She was napping on the floor, but her eyes popped open the instant he appeared at her side.

"The hell do you want?" she asked.

"I want the same thing you do," Seth said. "I want the darknet. I know what I need to get from it. Question is, what do you want out of it? Are you after the weapon?"

"I'm after all kinds of information. The darknet servers have private information on people you don't even know exist, who are running a lot of shit in the background of our world. I want to get up in that."

Seth wondered how she'd react if she knew that she wanted the servers for the same reason that Lucifer did. Dana hunted vampires—getting compared to one couldn't have been a compliment. "So you're not trying to find the ethereal plane that balefire comes from."

A smile spread across her round face. "Don't tell me *you* want balefire."

"I want to know how to get past it," Seth said. "How to control it, how to destroy it. Would that be on the darknet?"

She stood up slowly. "Maybe."

"Where did you expect to find the servers?"

"Free me and I'll show you," Dana said.

Seth grabbed her elbow and phased both of

them out.

He took a quick step back when they both reappeared in the courtyard above, far from the guards keeping the dungeon on lockdown. He expected Dana to attack him.

She only started walking.

Dana surprised him a second time by starting to talk while she headed deeper into the halls of Niflheimr. "I looked into the goat-woman thing for Marion."

"You said you didn't want to."

"I'm a sucker." She shrugged. "Actually, Penny's a sucker. She thinks I need to be nice to Marion. Anyway. What I found doesn't make any sense. There're not a lot of goat-type critters running around these days. None of the ones that are still alive could present any threat to Marion."

"What about dead ones?"

"There was one that hasn't been seen since Genesis," Dana said. "A librarian from Hell."

Seth's eyebrows lifted. "Hell librarian?"

"Laugh it up, but this librarian throws up all kinds of red flags. Her information's been stripped from every the database I know how to access. I only found out she exists because pre-Genesis diaries from Hell mention her. Her name's Onoskelis."

"We'll have to see if that rings any bells for Marion," Seth said.

"It won't. Bells wouldn't ring bells for Marion. She's not there anymore." Dana tapped her temple.

"Don't talk about her like that."

"You might think this braindead Marion is cute, and that's fine, but it's not Marion. Don't try to dispute me on this shit. You don't know my sister like I do."

"You've given up on her, so you can't know her that well."

"Blah, blah, blah," Dana said.

She was taking Seth down a familiar hallway —the same one where Marion had led him during the engagement party.

Dana stopped at the corner and peered around the side. "Shit. The Hardwicks' apartment is being guarded by Raven Knights."

That was easy enough to get past.

Seth grabbed her elbow and phased again.

They reappeared in the rooms past the guards. He'd taken care to materialize in the bathroom, just to be sure that they wouldn't get caught, but nobody was inside the room.

"The servers are in here?" Seth asked, stepping out of the bathroom.

Dana shoved past him. "The entrance to the server room should be. I've got a lot of triadist friends, and one of them told me that Pierce Hardwick had a secret passage."

She flung the pantry door open. There were still old utensils scattered across the dusty floor from when Marion had tripped. It had been too dark for Seth to see that one of the floor tiles was discolored in the back of the pantry, and set a few centimeters higher than the others.

No wonder Marion had tripped. She was ordinarily so graceful, it was hard to imagine she could have stumbled over her own feet.

Dana took a stone key out of a pouch on her belt and tapped it against the tile.

Unseelie magic flared. The tile melted away, revealing a tunnel underneath.

"Ta-da," she said. "You coming?"

Seth felt Lucifer's USB drive in his pants pocket. "Wouldn't miss it."

Dana dropped down first, and Seth followed second. It wasn't a long drop. The hallway underneath was darker and chillier than anywhere else he'd seen in the palace. It also branched off in three directions.

"This way." She led him down the left-hand hall. It was so long that it vanished into darkness. "Five miles that way, under the ocean, behind a big-ass door. That's where the servers are kept."

"Do you have a map?"

Dana pulled one out. It wasn't magical, like the one she'd loaned him for use in Sheol, but hand-drawn. It only showed the sub-level that they stood on. That was probably because the rest of Niflheimr was too complex to be mapped properly.

"Here's where we are." She pointed at one end. "And here's where the tunnel is."

Seth could visualize it, but he really hated teleporting places he'd never been before.

"All right." He took a bracing breath. "Let's do this."

He grabbed Dana's elbow a third time.

They phased.

And they reappeared without ground under their feet.

Seth didn't even have an instant to swear out loud before they plunged into black water so frigid that it should have been solid. But it wasn't. It consumed their bodies instantly.

Water flooded his nose and throat. It flooded the wound on his belly, exposed underneath the glamour, and blinded him with cold.

Dana's arm slipped out of his hand. The bubbles of her breath escaping her lungs slid past him, silver in the darkness.

Wearing stone armor made her drop fast.

Seth propelled himself toward her, feet kicking and arms outstretched. He had never tried to phase underwater before. He didn't know if attempting it would displace the water or if it would fill him—maybe even finish killing him.

He could only swim. Dana sank faster than he did, and the black water seemed bottomless.

She faded out of sight.

Seth kept swimming, kept pushing, even when his lungs strained for air. He couldn't give up. He couldn't tell Marion her sister was dead.

And then the water churned around him.

Dana reappeared, shoved upward by frothing sidhe magic. She caught him in hands gauntleted by stone, nearly wrenching the arms out of his sockets by the speed of her rise.

They erupted on the surface together. Their

gasps for air echoed into the lightless cavern.

"I'm sorry," Seth panted, treading water. Water plastered his shirt to his shoulders. His booted feet were sluggish. "I must have missed. The map—I'm bad with maps."

"You didn't miss." Dana sounded a hell of a lot calmer than he was. "Grab my belt and hold on." He did as instructed. She reengaged the sidhe magic, using it to push them across the surface of the water. "That five-mile tunnel was flooded halfway down. I'd planned to use these spells to get me to the surface before I ran out of air."

"You knew it was flooded? And you didn't tell me?"

"You didn't ask." Dana got them to a narrow stone platform and hauled herself out. She offered a hand to help Seth too, but he escaped on his own.

He lifted the hem of his shirt to check the wound. Water seemed to be seeping out of his skin, but he couldn't see any sign of additional fraying around the glamour.

"Your six pack is still intact," Dana said dryly, tossing a witchlight onto the ground between them. It lit up the disc of the floor they stood on— barely twelve feet in diameter—and a single computer workstation at its center. The light illuminated Dana from underneath her chin, casting long shadows onto her forehead that made her look downright demonic.

"This is the server?" Seth asked. The computer didn't look like it could host websites that caused as much trouble as those on the darknet.

She dropped into the chair and cracked her knuckles before resting her fingers on the keyboard. "It's just the access point." It looked like a normal computer, as far as Seth could tell—aside from its position under the ocean in the Winter Court. The monitor was old, probably almost as old as Genesis, and its cables led into the stone under their feet.

Dana pressed the power button.

Lights arced up the walls around them, which Seth hadn't been able to see until that moment. The cavern was wider than a football field and shaped like they were inside of an egg.

The walls were made entirely of servers.

"Oh my God," Seth said, turning where he stood. He gazed up at the flashing lights in shock. He'd never seen so much equipment before. It hummed like a snoring giant.

A login screen blinked to life on the monitor. Dana started typing.

"My wife's a computer nerd, so she just needs one special account on here to download all the data that's ever touched the servers," she explained. "And the security on the darknet systems isn't as good once you're in here because nobody should be able to get in, between the magical and physical barriers."

"Wait," Seth said.

He took the USB drive out of his pocket. It didn't look damaged, but he shook all the water out of it before plugging it into a port on the side of the monitor.

"What are you doing?" Dana asked.

A window popped up on the screen. Text scrolled quickly by. Seth didn't understand it, but he assumed it was Lucifer's program going to work. "I don't just want information on balefire. I promised a vampire that I'd get him access to the servers in exchange for getting turned."

"Turned? Into a *vampire*?" Disgust curled her upper lip. "Why in the hells would you want to do that?"

"I can't die," Seth said, patting his chest.

"Fuck that." She reached for the USB drive to unplug it, but Seth caught her wrist.

"Please," he said. "I need this."

"You don't want to be one of the bloodless. I hunt them for a reason. Being undead is miserable! And if you turn your avatar into some corpse, you might never die, and never go back to being God."

"That's kind of the point."

The chair's legs squealed as Dana pushed it back, standing up to stare Seth in the eye. "I can't believe you'd rather be a vampire than a god."

"If I become a vampire, I'd get to keep the life I've built," Seth said. "My life...and Marion."

Doubt flickered through Dana's eyes. "It's like that, huh?"

"She needs me right now. That's all I'm saying."

"You're fucking stupid," she said matter-of-factly. But she sat back down and didn't try to pull out the thumb drive. "Extra stupid because I can't find nothing about balefire while this program is running, and I can't give Penny a login either. Great job, Einstein."

"You can ask Lucifer for a login," Seth said. He doubted that Lucifer would give Dana anything, given her propensity for vampire slaying.

She seemed to take that as a challenge, though. Mirth smoldered in her eyes. "Sure. I can 'ask.'" Dana leaned back in the chair, folding her arms across her chest. "What are you going to do about my sister?"

"She asked me to reveal myself as God and endorse her wedding," Seth said.

"Will you do it?"

He ran a hand down his chest, feeling the convincing glamour Sinead McGrath had made for him. "If Lucifer changes me, I can't go around claiming I'm a god, can I?"

"Seems like you've got a problem, then," Dana said. "Because if you endorse Marion's wedding, she's gonna get married. But if you don't, you're gonna lose her even if you do become a vampire."

His mouth was dry. He swallowed hard. "Yeah. I know."

"Then it sounds like you've got a decision to make." She laughed. "Sucks to be you."

EIGHTEEN

Konig didn't return to Marion's bedroom after their fight. She didn't know if she should have been grateful for that or not.

The argument seemed like such a simple misunderstanding, requiring minimal explanation to sort things out. But she needed his patient attention in order to do that.

Marion could forgive him for the incident, if he'd forgive her for hurting him first.

It was all so *fixable*.

Wedding preparations churned on.

Heather retrieved Marion from bed at first light. "Can't sleep in on your wedding day," the archer said.

Marion hadn't slept at all. She'd spent the night hugging her pillow, watching the curtains flutter, and wondering if she'd made a mistake.

There hadn't been anything else she could do.

It was likely that she should have spent those hours talking with the council in order to squeeze a few last-minute votes in her direction, but she hadn't been able to move without grimacing. That last strike Konig had flung in her direction had left her badly bruised.

She kicked the sheets off. "Oh, thank you," she said when she realized Heather had brought breakfast in on a tray.

"You need your strength," Heather said.

"Not that I don't appreciate the gesture, but where's Nori? She usually assists me."

Heather shook her head. "Busy with other wedding stuff. I think she's assisting Konig today."

The mere mention of his name made Marion's stomach flip. She didn't have much of an appetite.

It wouldn't do to faint when she was walking down the aisle, though.

Marion ate on her balcony, where she could watch the rest of the Autumn Court bustling with activity. Security had tripled overnight. The forest outside her balcony teemed with people, most of them human-looking, though it was hard to tell preternaturals at that distance.

She could tell when the other guests began arriving from Earth specifically because security began swarming her lawn, forming rings of protection. They were sparing no expense to ensure Arawn couldn't reach her.

The guards shouldn't have worried. Arawn's people couldn't touch sunlight, and it was a sunny day in the Autumn Court. Nothing stood between Marion and her wedding with Konig.

Marion was safe. She had never been safer in her life.

Why did she feel so vulnerable?

"How are arrivals going?" Marion asked.

"Great. We've got every ley line wide open and everyone in the court is helping escort guests. You wouldn't believe who Violet managed to talk into attending." Heather ticked the list off of her fingers. "Actors, human politicians, the press, some great bloggers, sidhe from the other courts…"

"Lovely." None of those people were showing up for her. They were just there to see the event of the century. "I trust that there's no sign of danger if you're here with me."

"We'll know if anything happens. I've got all my people on the lookout." Heather leaned her elbow on the balcony, smiling down at Marion. "They'll be your people soon. You excited?"

"I am," Marion said. That wasn't even a lie. She'd soon be wearing the diadem of a queen, on a throne overlooking a mighty kingdom, and that was where she was meant to be.

Excitement wasn't her only emotion, though.

"These eggs are overcooked," Marion said.

Heather picked up the plate. "I'll have new ones made. Be right back."

As soon as she left, Marion went to the overnight bag she'd packed for the wedding. She had brought the bottle of water from Mnemosyne as an afterthought without expecting to need it. But now Marion was going to marry Konig, and she wanted to do it remembering everything.

Marion needed to remember how she'd loved him. Their first meeting, the first swoons of passion, their long nights together. Whispers shared one long day in Konig's bedroom weren't enough to comfort her anymore. She needed to become the old Marion again—the woman whom everyone hated.

Better hated by everyone than petrified of marrying Konig.

She twisted the cap off of the bottle. Seth had filled it to the point where the surface shivered a centimeter from the mouth.

"Please," Marion whispered, unsure of what she was asking for.

She drained the bottle, throat working, lungs tightening, heart pounding.

The memories seemed to radiate from her stomach where the water settled.

Marion remembered that garden again—that vast, blue-tinted expanse with trees thicker than any on Earth. She remembered running with a boy much older than her. Playing with him. Laughing.

She also remembered sitting beside a lake with Rylie. She remembered the Alpha sharing words of warning with her, though not the specific language. Rylie had looked stern. She had looked angry. And Marion remembered feeling surprised that Rylie could get that kind of angry, because

Marion had never seen her in such a mood before.

None of that was as important as the toddler that was seated beside Rylie's legs as she spoke. Like the teenager Marion had seen in the garden, he had soft black hair and brown skin.

The Wilder coloring, Marion now knew.

And she remembered dreams of war and fire, and standing among a field of bodies while feeling responsible for what had happened to them.

Those memories were things she'd remembered before—back when she'd touched Seth, skin to skin, before knowing he was Seth.

Some of the things the water of Mnemosyne made her remember were from that time, too.

Waking up in the Ransom Falls hospital with Seth's name on her lips.

The doctor, Lucas Flynn, remaining by her side through medical testing. His reassuring presence hadn't waned in the days that followed, like at the bookstore where the seller had hated preternaturals. Or when she had almost been killed by an assassin in the Autumn Court.

Seth was everywhere in her mind—filling every nook and cranny of who she was.

There was nothing from *before*.

Marion dropped the water bottle with a gasp, shocked back into her skin.

The river hadn't helped her remember because those memories had all been taken away, destroyed in the Canope. There was nothing to restore.

She didn't feel differently about Konig.

And she definitely didn't feel differently about Seth.

Heather knocked on the bedroom door. "I've got your eggs."

Marion swiped her hands over her cheeks, rubbing away moisture. Then she tossed the bottle into the recycling. "Come in."

The archer brought eggs that were slightly runny, which was perfect. They didn't look remotely appetizing.

"Better?" Heather asked.

"I've changed my mind," Marion said. "Bring in the stylists. I want to get dressed now."

There was no point delaying the inevitable.

"Tip your head," said the hairstylist. Marion obediently did as told, allowing her hair to spill down her back.

The stylist was one of a dozen attendants working on Marion in a flurry of wild activity. They were tugging on her hair, brushing makeup over her eyes, concealing tiny blemishes on her chin.

At some point, she'd been instructed to step into fancy underwear, and she had. They hadn't been able to cinch it yet. They were waiting on a healer to repair the bruising that Konig had delivered the night before. Nobody had asked how she'd been injured. They'd just seen the mottled markings and called for a witch.

Once she was healed, the dress itself would come next.

"I don't feel well," Marion said, pressing a hand to her stomach. "I think I'm going to throw up."

"That's normal." Heather reclined with her boots propped up on the vanity, still wearing the Hound-hide trousers. "Everyone feels like that when they're about to get married."

"I suppose that's true."

"Chin up." Nori's tone was a little too sharp to be consoling. She'd arrived to help dressed in the gown selected for Marion's bridal party, which was an icy shade of blue to honor the Winter Court. "You're about to marry the most desirable member of the sidhe royal families. You've got nothing to be nervous about."

"Also true," Marion said, even more faintly than before.

The hairstylist tugged too hard on her curls. Tears sprang to her eyes.

Marion wished she'd had a friend with her—someone who she could tell about what happened with Konig. It wasn't like Heather would side with Marion. Heather had been guarding Konig since the two of them had been toddlers.

If Marion's mother had been there... Or even Dana...

But not a single person that she could describe as a friend was going to attend the wedding, much less help her prepare for it. She had to sit there, surrounded by stylists assigned by her soon-to-be mother-in-law, unable to say a single word crossing her mind.

A tear escaped to slide down her cheek.

"Don't do that," said the sidhe doing her makeup. "You're going to destroy the mascara."

Marion stood suddenly. The chair swiveled, its arms knocking into her stylists.

Her reflection in the elaborate underwear and makeup was stunning—exactly the way she'd want to look on her wedding night, her first evening shared with her husband.

She wanted to leap off of the nearest waterfall into a chasm.

"I need to be alone," Marion said.

Nori checked her watch. "You have to start pre-ceremony press soon. We've booked an exclusive interview with January Lazar to precede the council's vote, and then you've got about fifteen minutes to relocate to the venue for the ceremony..."

And that was assuming the ceremony would happen at all. Everything hinged on the vote.

Marion fought to swallow down the burning in her throat. "Yes, I know I have a tight schedule. That's why I need a few minutes to myself *now*." Imperiousness crept into her tone, and she embraced it—the one thing that might protect her. "I'm not making a request. Empty my rooms!"

She barely heard the sullen muttering from her stylists. She stormed to the balcony doors and glared out at the bright sky as they left. She blinked rapidly, trying to keep tears from sliding down her cheeks.

It wouldn't do to ruin the stupid *makeup*.

As soon as her room was empty, she whipped away from the window, pacing across her room. She tried to take a few deep breaths to calm herself. She couldn't inhale without her back hurting. Marion suspected that Konig had broken a rib when he'd thrown her.

"Get it together," Marion hissed at herself, leaning on the vanity so she could glare at her beautiful reflection in the mirror. "Chin up. Stop weeping. You can do this!"

Motion stirred in the mirror over her shoulder.

She straightened, prepared to snap at whoever dared to intrude.

And then Marion saw Seth's face.

He stepped out of the shadows by the closet. Light glimmered under his shirt, and it wasn't as faint as it had been the night before. His wound must have been expanding around the edges of the glamour.

"Are you okay?" Marion asked, leaning back against the vanity. It was as much distance as she could put between them without going onto the balcony.

He smoothed a hand down the front of his shirt. "Aside from a near-drowning, yes. It was my fault. I wasn't prepared for where I'd find the darknet servers."

"They're *underwater*?" It certainly explained why she hadn't been able to find them before. "At least you're okay. Thank the gods—or thank *you*, I suppose. You should have been more careful."

He wasn't looking at her. "You might want to, uh…"

"What?" She looked down at herself. She was still wearing nothing but the underwear. "Oh, for heaven's sake." She took the silk robe off of her vanity and covered herself. "How did you find the servers?"

"Dana helped me. Oh, and I released her back to Vegas. Sorry."

Marion might have been annoyed a few hours earlier, before Konig had visited her. Now she only felt numb. "That's fine. I don't care."

Seth took a step toward her.

She jerked back reflexively, nearly knocking her makeup off of the vanity.

The clatter stopped him in his tracks. He hung back, confused. And why wouldn't he? As Konig had pointed out, Marion had been dragging Seth off to shadowy corners the night before. Now she was trying to escape him. Talk about mixed signals.

Marion lifted her chin, reassuming her shield of arrogance. "Shouldn't you be seeing Lucifer so that you can become a vampire now?"

"I wanted to talk to you first," Seth said.

His tone was so much gentler than hers. If he'd gotten angry, she could have shoved him away, yelled at him to leave her room. But his calm wormed its way through her defenses like they weren't even there. "What do you need?"

"You asked me to give a speech to endorse your wedding. The thing is, if I tell everyone I'm God, I'm going to have to be God. I'll be shouldering all the responsibility that entails. I'll be blamed for Genesis."

He wanted to talk about Genesis now? Of all times? Marion couldn't have cared less about any apocalypse, past or future. "I already told you that it's fine if you don't want to talk to the council. I'm sure Violet hasn't slept a wink all night so that she could convince everyone to agree with us. I've the best sidhe politicians on my side. You don't owe me anything."

"I just think I'd be more helpful if I get turned into a vampire," Seth said.

"You'll have to walk me through the logic. I don't understand."

"If I become godly, I'll be detached from this life. But if I become a vampire...I could stay." He took one small step closer, as cautious as though approaching a wounded bird. "I could stay with you, Marion."

Seth wasn't sure how he had expected Marion to react to his offer. He knew he hadn't expected her to laugh, though.

It was almost shrill, and that sounded so strange coming from her, especially now that she had on such careful makeup and her hair half-done. She looked like a supermodel who had been hired to play a queen in a movie, rather than a woman who was actually going to become a queen. Yet she laughed shrilly, a little hysterically, and it sounded *wrong*.

"Stay with me," she said, dabbing under her eyes with her fingertips. "As a vampire."

"Well, vampires don't get along with sunlight, and there's no sun in the Winter Court," Seth said slowly. "I could stick around to defend you from Leliel, or whoever else attacks if Niflheimr's wards fall. I mean, even if Konig gets his title stripped—you could still be safe, Marion. I'd protect you."

She just kept laughing. Her shoulders shook, and then her whole body shook, and she covered her face with both hands.

It took a few seconds for her to stop trembling.

When her hands dropped again, she straightened her spine and her face was blank.

"I won't need a vampire to guard me," Marion said with strange detachment. "I'm going to marry Konig. He'll be able to restore the wards even if his title is stripped, and we'll handle Leliel when she comes." Even when she was icy, she was beautiful. Maybe *especially* when she was icy.

Seth didn't like her as much like this, with her hair twisted atop her head, and so much makeup he couldn't see the texture of her flawless skin. He didn't like when she smiled like she was hiding anger.

She'd been so different the night before.

Something was wrong.

"Talk to me," Seth said. "I don't have angel mind-reading powers. What's going on in your head?"

She turned from him with a twist of her shoulders that all but screamed dismissiveness. "Go see Lucifer. It takes time to be transformed into a vampire, so you'll want to start soon." When she faced the window, the bright light spilled over one shoulder, highlighting the nape of her neck and fine hairs that hadn't yet been pinned into place.

The skin was bruised. It looked like fingerprints.

Marion's chilliness must have been contagious. It felt like the icy spires of Niflheimr had just taken up residence within Seth's gut.

"Take off the robe," Seth said.

She went rigid. "What?"

"The robe," he said. "Drop it."

Marion clutched it at her chest. "*Excuse* me. I'm getting married!"

"Don't try to distract me. Let me see your back. You're wounded."

Her carefully constructed mask cracked. Her bottom lip trembled. "But Seth..." She didn't move away when he approached her this time.

"Please?" Seth asked.

Marion nodded mutely, and she turned away from him again, letting the robe fall into the crooks of her elbows.

At another time, Seth would have been distracted by her spine's graceful furrow dipping behind the laces of her loose corset. The blue-white of her undergarments offset her olive skin tones perfectly.

It also drew out the blue in her bruises.

Numerous markings mottled the skin he could see—and that was only what was exposed.

"Can I...?" he asked, tugging on the bow.

She nodded again without looking at him.

He unknotted the corset and slid a finger underneath the laces to loosen them. It fell apart under his hands, exposing a thin chemise underneath, which was little more than tissue.

Seth lifted it to see the damage.

And that was the only word for it. Damage.

Seth skimmed his palm over the bruises. They covered more space than his hands could with fingers spread. She shivered at the contact. "Did this happen when we fell in the pantry?"

"No, it wasn't the fall." She let the robe tumble completely off of one arm and showed it to him. It was definitely fingerprints on her smooth flesh. Someone had grabbed her hard—someone with a hand the size of an adult man's.

Seth could only think of one man that Marion would allow close enough to do that.

"Konig?" The name came out flat, like death on his lips.

A tear slid down Marion's cheek. She'd never been laughing. She had been trying not to cry.

Seth folded Marion into his arms, burying his nose in her hair, inhaling the scent of lavender and burned oak. A scent that was now as familiar to him as fresh-cut grass, and just as comforting.

Holding her was the only thing that kept the white light of rage from carrying Seth out of Marion's bedroom to smear Konig's pretty boy-band face across the throne room floor. But he couldn't even hold her as tight as he wanted. Not without hurting her.

"What do you want to do about him?" Seth asked.

Marion's fingers squeezed his arms. "What do *I* want to do?"

"I already know what I'd want to do to Konig." Seth was having incredibly colorful thoughts about murdering Konig right at that moment—far from his typical thought processes, but irrepressible nonetheless. "What I want doesn't matter, though. Tell me what needs to happen and I'll make it happen."

"Well," Marion said, audibly swallowing, "I have to marry Konig."

Seth took her gently by the upper arms, pushing her far enough back that he could see her. Her makeup was streaky. Her eyes were puffy. "You don't *have* to do anything. Say the word and I'll take you far away. Anywhere you want."

"You don't understand. I *want* to do this." She managed to say that with conviction even though she was still crying. "I won't be Queen of the Winter Court if I don't." Her voice hitched. She scrubbed a hand over her eyes, smearing the makeup further. "And I love Konig."

Of all the things she could have said, none

shocked him as much as that. "He beat the crap out of you."

"It was my fault. He heard that you and I were sneaking around last night and he thought..." Marion flinched as though she'd been hit all over again. "He got jealous."

Seth searched for words and found none.

He gently sat Marion in front of the vanity, and then paced the room, seeking an outlet for that anger that didn't involve throttling Konig. "Let's say you were cheating on him with me. Or anyone else. Do you think that means you'd deserve to get hit?"

"Jealousy makes people irrational, and I've been getting on every one of Konig's last nerves. I've been distant from him since I lost my memory. I haven't..." She clapped a hand over her mouth, and she said, very quietly, "We haven't been having sex. And he's sidhe. It's worse than hitting Konig."

"No, as a matter of fact, it is fucking *not*," Seth said.

"Konig and I haven't been sleeping together. What is he supposed to think when you and I are seen...?" Her eyes flicked up to him, and then back down to her hands. Marion shook her head. "I hurt him long before he hurt me."

"That's bullshit. Jesus, Marion. This isn't the ferocious woman I know talking. The woman who bullied me all the way up the Pacific Northwest, laid claim to my bank account, and invited herself on my trip to Sheol. What happened to *that* woman? The one entitled to whatever she wants?"

"She got everyone killed!" Marion cried out with sudden, shocking fierceness. "Don't you realize, Seth? I was selfish and entitled and the refugees were killed!" He opened his mouth. She didn't let him speak. "I'm a horrible person and everyone knows that. My own mother won't be at the wedding!"

He dropped to his knees in front of her, clutching her hands. "Listen. We don't hit the people we love. There is *no excuse*. Ever." Seth swallowed down the knot in his throat. "I would never hurt you, Marion." He pressed his forehead to hers. "Look inside. Read my mind."

She pulled away without searching his thoughts. "How can you say that? You drank my blood in Sheol long before Konig ever struck me."

A chill settled over Seth.

"It's different," he said hoarsely.

But is it?

"I can't be selfish," Marion said again firmly, if not fiercely. "This wedding needs to happen."

"If he's done this once, he'll do it again. It'll only escalate." Seth backed away, resisting the urge to touch her. "Let me take you out of here. If you don't trust me either, if you want me to go away too—okay, I'll drop you off and leave. I'd rather you feel safe than have you martyr yourself to become queen."

She pulled the robe around herself, grabbed a tissue, and started wiping off her ruined makeup. There was another bruise on her cheekbone that had been covered with foundation. "I do want your help. Promise you'll help me."

"Anything," Seth said.

"Go in front of the council and tell them you're God. Endorse my wedding. Ensure I get the votes I need. That's the best way to protect my interests right now."

"Your interests?" Seth asked. "What about *you*?"

The door to the hallway started to open. Voices echoed into the bedroom. It was Marion's people, presumably on the way to finish dressing her for the wedding.

"Serve me, Seth," Marion said. "You said you'd do anything, and this is what I want."

He wasn't going to defy her. He'd do what she asked, because he was better than Konig. He owed her that much.

But it still hurt to phase out of the room before Marion's entourage could see him.

NINETEEN

The final preparations took little time. Marion was healed by a sidhe with a few twists of magic. Then she stepped into her wedding dress and the bodice was cinched tightly. Metal jingled softly as the toggles for her dress were pressed into place. Cold diamonds kissed her chest. The roots of her hair were yanked.

Her schedule was running through her mind as though shouted by someone at her back, trying to drown out every other thought, and every warm-eyed, scar-lipped face gazing at her.

She had to do a lot of photos before the ceremony. Hours of them.

And then...the vote.

Jibril would deliver the vote as proxy, but Marion would accomplish nothing else while that was happening. She'd be getting photographed, surrounded by attendants and the Raven Knights, when she found out if Konig would remain prince.

They would win. Seth was going to stand up for her, so they had no alternative but to win.

She'd be married by the time night fell.

Marion snapped out of the depths of thought when her attendants began murmuring. Several stepped away to bow.

The Onyx Queen entered.

She was dressed in darker colors than usual to provide contrast to the bride in white: rich ambers touched with ruby. Strings of pearls had been replaced by roses in her hair. A gold crescent dangled between her eyebrows.

Violet carried a large box in her arms like a baby as she approached, smiling for Marion. The expression didn't touch her empty eyes.

"Your Highness." Marion curtsied.

"Queens don't bow to one another." Violet reached up to touch her curls. The smile softened around the edges, becoming more genuine. "You look lovely."

Your son hit me.

"Thank you," she said.

"I've brought a final accent piece for your wedding dress," Violet said. "I think you'll like this one." She lifted the lid of the box to reveal Marion's bow nestled alongside her quiver. They glimmered with new enchantments. "I cast spells of unbreaking on these myself."

The magic was far more elaborate than anything Marion could dream of casting. People would have paid their life's savings for such enchantments and still been unable to afford them.

"It's beautiful," Marion said.

"And intimidating. I want everyone to know that you can defend yourself. May I?"

Marion nodded. Violet slung the bow over her back and used the belt to hang the quiver. Everything was white and bejeweled. They matched the wedding dress surprisingly well.

"I'm a mage," Marion said. "I don't need physical weapons, in theory. I like it, though." She was weirdly touched by the gesture. It was the one element in her entire wedding that seemed tailored to Marion rather than the sidhe in general.

Violet clasped her hands. "Remember this: Blessing as it may be, marriage is a battlefield. You'll have to fight to become better than your nature. Konig will have to do the same. If you win, you'll be rewarded in partnership for the rest of your life."

Marion's smile slipped. "Thank you."

"I'll see you at the wedding." Violet patted her cheek and left.

Her cheek was cold where the queen had touched her. Marion brushed her fingers over the spot.

Was Konig worth fighting for?

Heather stepped up onto the platform with Marion. "Warn me if you think you're going to faint," she said kindly. "I'll catch you so you don't fall on your own arrows."

"I'm not going to faint."

"Good, because it's time to start walking." Heather offered a hand to help Marion down to the floor.

Marion was dressed. Mentally, she hadn't been present for the process, but she hadn't needed to be.

She took a moment to survey her regal reflection. Queenly, indeed. A few touches of color had been added so she wouldn't be so pale against the vivid Autumn Court—some emeralds, some sapphires—but she still looked like icy perfection.

The spray of glittery jewels upon her hair almost made it seem like she'd died among the Winter Court's snow and was freezing over.

"If you're looking for the diadem, you won't be wearing it in the first pictures." Nori had been managing all of the preparations and barely looked up from her clipboard. "You'll get it right before the ceremony to surprise everyone."

Marion hadn't been worried. She didn't care.

At least it didn't feel like she was going to cry anymore.

She took Heather's hand and stepped down. Even the archer was dressed for the ceremony, though her idea of formal involved the Hound-hide breeches and a prettier bow than usual. Hers was still more utilitarian than Marion's. There was no attempt to mask Heather's function as killer-on-hand for the bride.

Marion felt like she was drifting in slow

motion on her way to take photographs. The wedding photographer was already present and must have been there the entire time she was dressing. The camera, heavily warded against the energy of the Middle Worlds, flashed as it snapped shots of her journey.

What kind of images would it capture? A blushing bride waiting to meet her groom?

It couldn't capture any bruises. They were already gone.

It couldn't capture the tumult within her mind. *In her mind.*

Seth had pressed his forehead to hers, urging her to read his mind. To see the truth.

What truth? That he wouldn't hurt her?

That their feelings went far beyond what a god and the Voice should share?

Marion was taken to the atrium. She was posed. She held the positions, and they took more photos.

Seth would be going to the council now to give his speech.

He was going to endorse Konig.

He'd offered to take her away, anywhere she wanted—somewhere that she could be safe from Konig.

But Marion shouldn't have needed to be safe. She'd said it herself: Konig loved her, even if he had lied about Charity's death. What else could he have been lying about? There was no way to know. She couldn't read the mind of a sidhe prince without his permission.

She recalled Seth pressing his forehead to hers again—and then when Ymir, the little frost giant, had pointed to his forehead in the Niflheimr dressing room.

Ymir had witnessed Leliel's attack. He'd been telling Marion to read his mind.

"Nori," Marion said abruptly.

The photographer gave a cry of protest. "You ruined the shot!"

"Wait for a few minutes." Marion waved him off and searched her party for Nori. The other half-angel was standing in back, as if avoiding pictures. "Nori! Can I talk to you?"

Uneasily, Nori edged over. "We don't have a lot of time."

"Forget about time." Marion's mind had kicked into high gear. "I need you to find Ymir for me. He was there when Leliel attacked the Winter Court."

"So was I. What about it?"

"Did you see what happened to Charity?"

"Charity Ballard? The revenant nurse?" Nori's lips had gone colorless. "We told you, she died."

"But did you see her die? Because Seth says she's not dead. He can feel her life out there." Marion led Nori further away, behind the veil of vines hanging from the corner. It was bright, even there. The Autumn Court was a shining jewel at midday. "I want to talk to another witness of Leliel's attack."

"Ymir hasn't been talking," Nori said. "I think the trauma, you know...it muted him."

"I don't need him to talk with words."

Nori set her clipboard on the windowsill slowly. "It'll take a few minutes for me to dig him out of Niflheimr and bring him over—he's been hiding a lot lately, and—"

"Just find him. I need to see him before I can walk down the aisle." Before she swore her undying, eternal love to Konig.

"This isn't the time, Marion," Nori said.

"It's the only time. Can you help me?"

Nori took a long time to nod, but she did. "I'll be as fast as I can."

Marion could have cried from gratitude, but that would have gotten her in trouble with the makeup artists. She settled for giving Nori a quick hug.

And then her cousin left to find Ymir.

Marion didn't immediately emerge from the vines. She leaned against the wall, shut her eyes, took a few deep breaths. She had been sleepwalking through everything since Seth had left her, and now it was time to stop and focus.

"How are you holding up?" Heather asked, joining her.

Marion was too emotionally blasted to be anything but honest. "I've been better."

"You're right to be worried about Arawn," Heather said. "You can trust that I won't let anything happen. Look there, and there." She pointed. Trees curved away from the windows outside. "Magically regrown to make sure the sun can reach all corners of Myrkheimr. And then look over there." She pointed again.

Marion's eyes saw nothing when she focused on the wall that Heather indicated. Her senses felt something else. "New wards."

"Set to trigger physical attacks when tripped. We've got lights everywhere. Electricity too. We'll be able to blast the shit out of any demon that tries to ruin your wedding, princess."

"That makes me feel better," Marion lied, offering a tremulous smile to Heather.

"It should," Heather said. "Trust me when I say that nothing will stop this wedding from happening. Nothing."

Elsewhere in Myrkheimr, the members of the council gathered for the vote.

The open-walled suite was at the base of a waterfall, which cast everything in a damp amber haze. A glittering river wrapped around the entire room like a moat, and Seth's skin buzzed when he stepped over a bridge to enter. It let him pass, but not before sweeping every atom of his body.

The glamour charm blinked at the ward's sweep, bright enough that all the guards noticed.

Every archer turned his way. A dozen of them. Their nocked arrows were anointed with something that gleamed toxic green.

He heard one mutter to another, "It's here."

The archers on the other side of the bridge stopped him.

"Arms up, legs spread," said a man.

Seth did as ordered. They patted him down, found both guns, and checked the magazines. He hadn't brought iron bullets. The sidhe gave both weapons back.

"You're good to go," said the other archer.

Once he had the attention of the security details, the council started looking his way, too. They were situated on low-slung wooden chairs and stone benches. Many of them already held glasses of wine, ready for unseelie festivities to come. Or perhaps drinking while wine was still offered, because it certainly would stop flowing if Konig's title got stripped.

Everyone in the room looked at Seth, one by one, and their expressions changed.

Word had gotten out about Dana's accusation. They all knew what he was purported to be.

God, even Rylie looked at him differently. But that probably had less to do with his status and more to do with what he'd let slip about Marion.

Konig wasn't among the council yet. In fact, Seth recognized nobody except Rylie—and Lucifer, whose crimson eyes lit up at the sight of Seth. He was shrouded in a hooded sweater that was wholly inappropriate for a wedding, particularly one in a location as lush as the Autumn Court.

Lucifer slithered through the crowd toward Seth. "Merry, meet Mr. Wilder."

"Not now," Seth said through his teeth.

"If not now, then when?" Lucifer fell into step

alongside him. "When you came asking for my help, you neglected to mention that you're a god."

"Leave me alone. Last warning."

"I wouldn't talk to me like that if I were you," Lucifer said. "I still have something you want, and now I realize its value is higher than I'd ever dreamed."

Of all the irritations that Seth was prepared to face at that moment, Lucifer's was not among them. Endless life seemed trivial in the face of what he was supposed to do.

"I got you what you want," Seth said. "You owe me blood now."

"Now? Right now? How do you think you'll prove what they're claiming you are if I change you?" Lucifer clearly meant that to be a hypothetical, because he grinned when he said it. "On a more interesting note, the data's decrypting. I see that you didn't delete information on that ethereal dimension."

"I didn't have time. Are you going to make me regret that?"

"You can delete all you want when I drain your blood," Lucifer said.

There was something in his tone that screamed of lies. But this wasn't Seth's first deal with the devil. He'd get what he wanted from Lucifer.

He just wasn't sure that he still wanted to be changed.

One woman broke away from the rest to stride toward Seth with fearless confidence. She thrust her hand toward him. "Deirdre Tombs. American Gaean Commission."

Seth already knew. He'd seen her shooting Rylie in the head. "Seth Wilder. God."

Lucifer laughed as he walked away.

"That's what I've heard." Deirdre didn't drop his hand. She squeezed as hard as he did. "I didn't see you."

"I don't follow."

"I'm a phoenix. I've died a few times. I've seen the gods on the other side of life, and you weren't with them." Her fingers tightened until her nails dug into the back of his hand.

"I've been AWOL," Seth said.

"What would motivate a guy to pretend to be a god, hypothetically speaking?" Deirdre asked.

Seth dropped her hand first, and he could tell she thought that was a victory. "You'd have to ask a guy pretending to be god."

She leaned in to whisper to him, "Did you have a nice time alone with Marion last night?"

He jerked back.

Deirdre had been spying on him.

"What do you want?" Seth asked.

"I've heard you're giving a speech to endorse the marriage today," Deirdre said. "Because the words of gods should calm the nerves of a lot of voters. Right? As long as you're a god, that is."

The mere mention of the endorsement he was meant to give flooded him with hot anger all over again.

Seth had been trying not to visualize Marion's

bruising because it had a way of overwhelming him. But even when he wasn't thinking about what Konig had done to her, he was still thinking about her crying in his arms, and the wet spots that had remained on his chest when he walked away.

"Nothing to say to defend yourself?" Deirdre asked.

"You haven't made any accusations." He brushed her off and walked to the edge of the central fire pit. Flame glimmered across the surface of crystals, generating just enough heat to offset the chill of the waterfall.

It shocked him that Deirdre went to sit by Rylie. Even more shocking when the Alpha didn't move away.

Seth might have interceded if Prince ErlKonig of the Autumn Court hadn't swaggered into the room at that moment, attended by another handful of Raven Knights.

It was sickening that Konig could be drenched in charismatic confidence when Seth had left Marion crying in her room.

The man was dressed for his wedding. White suit. Some leather things. Snowy patterns. He'd match Marion perfectly.

Seth wanted to kill him.

The intensity of the emotion was shocking. Seth's brother used to tease him for how easily he backed down from fights, and now he was contemplating murder.

Abel had never hit Rylie. Not once. And Abel

was the biggest douchebag to saunter across the face of the Earth.

"I haven't missed anything, have I?" Konig asked, flopping on an empty couch and throwing his leg over the back of it.

Seth was feeling so very vengeful at the moment.

"Not yet," Rylie said. Like always, she didn't have to speak up in order to be heard. As soon as she started talking, people fell quiet in order to listen. "Everyone knows why we're here, so I'll spare us any speeches. I want to remind you all that we aren't dealing with mere politics here. Our vote will shape the life of a pair of kids—young adults—who are very much in love."

She looked at Seth when she said that part.

Who was she reminding? The council, or him?

"I'd like to say something too." This came from Deirdre Tombs. "The lives of a pair who are 'very much in love' are nothing compared to what's at stake. This could impact the entire world."

"Possibly," said Adàn Pedregon. Seth recognized him from the news. "It'll only impact the whole world if their union stirs the gods to revenge."

And everyone looked at Seth again.

This was where he was supposed to endorse Marion and Konig's marriage.

Seth had made a promise to Marion. He'd said he would do anything she wanted.

Everyone was still looking at him, and he wasn't talking, and he didn't even know what he wanted to say.

Seth took a folded piece of paper out of his back pocket. He'd made a few notes on things he could say. Like Rylie, he didn't come from a background involving leadership; unlike Rylie, he hadn't spent the last twenty years developing those skills. His brain had a habit of going blank when the pressure was on. Werewolf hunter instincts couldn't make him a man of words.

At the moment, he couldn't even read what he'd written down.

When he looked at the page, all he saw was Marion's bruised back and her tearful face.

He crumpled the paper and tossed it in the fire.

"You all know who I am," Seth said. "And—"

"Do we?" Deirdre interrupted.

"He doesn't look like much of a god." That came from the man representing the Office of Preternatural Affairs. He was a tall, broad-shouldered human wearing a suit without a tie. The open collar gapped around the hollow of his throat.

Someone else whispered something like, "Avatar."

But people didn't look more convinced.

"Yes, I'm the avatar of the third god of the triad," Seth said reluctantly. "The demon god who's meant to rule death."

"You're not Arawn," said Ruelle Myön of the Allied Covens. Another face that Seth knew from the news. The last time that he'd seen her, she had been receiving oral favors from an unseelie waiter.

"Arawn's not the god of death. He's just pretending to make himself look cool." Konig yawned into his fist. "I beat the guy one-on-one. We don't need to worry about him."

Arawn wasn't the only one that had been beaten by Konig one-on-one.

Seth ripped the glamour off, snapping the cord that held it around his neck.

"I *am* Death," he said.

He tore his shirt from neck to hem and dropped it.

With the glamour gone, there was nothing to keep the illusion of skin from vanishing, exposing his innards.

The tearing had gotten worse. His breastbone was exposed now, as well as the pounding heart behind it. Every single squeeze of the muscle made foggy, electric energy bloom from the wound.

Seth didn't fight it for once. He embraced the godly energy, letting it fill him, flow from his fingertips, burn in his veins. "I am Death," he said again, turning to take in the whole room, fists clenched at his sides. "As a human avatar, I speak for myself and all the gods."

Nobody was arguing with him now.

There was silence in the room, as though everyone held their breaths.

Konig was smirking at Seth. His chin rested on his hand, legs crossed at the ankles. He was waiting for Seth to drop the bomb: the endorsement that would ensure Konig controlled

Marion, the Winter Court, and the darknet for decades to come.

"Our Voice said it at the summit, and I'll say it again." Seth towered over Konig, and he put to words what he couldn't do with fists. "There will be no angels in the Winter Court and we'll enforce it with blood. Vote to remove ErlKonig from the Autumn Court. Vote against the wedding." He glared at Konig as the prince's face drained of blood. "You will *never* touch Marion again."

TWENTY

Konig had thought he'd known anger when Marion had been mouthing off at him the night before. It had felt as though the wine had been a dark spirit possessing him. Everything his parents had ever told him about how to treat a woman— all those words about consent, respect, love—had been gone.

And he'd been strong.

Konig knew how to make Marion respect him. He'd seen the change in her face when he'd lashed out with magic. He'd been angry, and it had been so *righteous*.

There was nothing righteous about the anger he felt now.

Seth Wilder towered over him looking every inch the god—so much more than Arawn had as an impotent demon king in Sheol.

"You will *never* touch Marion again."

Konig had walked into the room with such confidence, sure he was on the brink of his wedding, and his coronation. The ascension from prince to king.

Seth stole that from him with a handful of ugly words.

Worse, Seth was telling Konig what he was allowed to do with Marion. *His* Marion. His woman, his bride, his princess.

Konig sat up slowly. It required pushing against the full force of Seth's energy to do it.

Avatar of god or not, Seth was still a man for the time being.

"What did you say?" Konig's words were chased by all the sidhe power that he normally held back for the benefit of mortals. It oozed from him. It twisted the hall.

Seth didn't repeat himself. "On your feet."

"Traitor," he hissed under his breath.

"We should vote now." That was Rylie speaking from the other couch. Konig could barely hear her under the throb of sidhe energy whining like a badly tuned cello. "Raise your hands if you are in favor of stripping Prince ErlKonig of his title."

Konig didn't look to see who raised their hands. He couldn't tear his eyes from the endless, inky pits of Seth's. Konig could see right through Seth's skull into whirling infinity. Endless stars. Distant suns.

A thousand-million deaths.

"Four," Rylie said. "Four votes."

Konig's heart sank, but still he couldn't look away.

Only four people voted in my favor?

He heard Deirdre Tombs's shout of dismay, though. "That's not possible! The votes—"

"We can't vote again," Rylie said. "It's settled. ErlKonig will remain Prince of the Autumn Court, and the wedding's on."

Seth turned, shocked. "What?"

Konig hadn't lost the vote.

He'd won.

To say that chaos erupted when the verdict was announced would have been an understatement.

Deirdre Tombs drew a gun.

Several people began to shapeshift.

The Raven Knights swarmed.

Seth rounded on Konig, and whatever shreds of humanity had remained in him were gone, utterly gone, stripped away to bare raw vengeance.

Konig's survival instinct kicked in at the sight of Seth's wrath. He'd seen death in those black eyes—a willingness to kill. He reached his mind into the ley lines, extended his body through them, and teleported away.

He phased into the throne room. That alone was adequate verification that Konig had kept his title. It was a protected area separate from the rest of Myrkheimr, and cocooned in so many wards that a wayward sidhe would have been shredded. None but the royal family and their closest servants could leap in there.

He landed safely, stumbling between his parents' thrones. His heart was pounding wildly.

Konig spun on the spot, looking around the shadowy throne room. The curtains had been drawn to conceal it from the rest of the kingdom, permitting not even the thinnest sliver of sunlight to touch the floor. It was also empty. There was nobody there to see his cowardly flight from Seth.

That was fine. Seth had lost the vote and Konig had won the war. He was still prince.

Amazing how quickly anger and fear turned into victory.

He thrust his fist into the air. "Yes!"

"It was Adàn Pedregon." Nori appeared moments after he did, breathless and flushed. She had been given authority to access the throne room when she was serving as diplomat for the angels, and it didn't seem to have been revoked. "I couldn't tell you before—I've been busy—but *Los Cambiaformas Internacional* has been pulling strings. Plus Deirdre did such a good job convincing everyone that Seth isn't a god because she thought he'd vouch for you—"

"You saw the vote?" Konig whirled her into his arms, planting a hard kiss on her mouth. He laughed wildly. "You saw the vote! You saw my victory!"

"*Our* victory."

"Yes, that's what I meant." Semantics. He was still prince, and he was about to become king.

"It's going to be a short win if we don't do something about Marion. That's why I came looking for you. Marion wants me to find Ymir before she walks down the aisle."

As high as he'd gone with the excitement, it took him a moment to crash back down again as the implications set in. Konig's shoulders tightened so hard that they shook. "What did you tell her?"

"I said I'd try. What was I supposed to say?"

"You should have put her off," he said. "You should have made her realize she needs to trust me."

"But how? It's not like she *can*. We're lying. She knows it. How can she trust that?" Each word made her voice rise in pitch until she was all but shrieking, loudly enough that people would be able to hear outside.

Konig wanted to slap her hard enough to shut her mouth, but Nori wasn't the same kind of beast as Marion, to be urged forward by spurs. She needed coaxing.

"Marion won't marry me if she knows what I've done to Ymir. Niflheimr will fall and you and I will lose our path to power. She absolutely cannot see him." Konig watched her face, waiting to see if she'd come to the right conclusion on her own. She kept looking charmingly befuddled. He had to fill her in. "Kill the kid. Tell Marion that Arawn did it because she left the Winter Court unprotected. She'll be too busy beating herself up to question it."

"I'm not going to kill a child!"

"Do you want to lose everything we've been working for, now that we're on the brink of victory?" His thumb skimmed over her bottom lip. "I'm so close. *We're* so close. I can taste it."

She opened her mouth to respond, but no words came out.

Her body jerked. She grunted. Her eyes widened.

A blade thrust through her belly.

Another jerk, and it cut upwards through her body, shredding her dress.

Nori fell.

Arawn stood behind her, yanking the sword free of her body. His hand was drenched in shiny half-angel blood.

⁂

The stylists were retouching Marion's makeup when news of the vote arrived. "We won!" Heather cried, bursting into the room. She was grinning with the triumph of it. Marion had never seen her smile like that before. "Only four people voted against us! Four!"

Seth must have advocated for Konig. Marion's plan had worked, and Konig was still prince.

"Those are great results," she said, moving her lips as little as possible. A makeup artist was brushing powder along her jawline.

Why was she so dead on the inside?

Heather slid onto the stool beside Marion's. "Not to be a pessimist, but I really hadn't expected that."

"I had a secret weapon on my side." Marion's tone was as empty as she felt. "Seth's a god. I asked him to stand up for us."

"You did? That's weird, because the doctor didn't 'stand up' for you at all. He practically threatened to rain hellfire if people voted in your favor, and the vote *still* didn't go that way. Everyone's talking about it."

The feelings that blossomed inside of Marion were so strange.

Despair. Horror. Anger.

Delight.

Seth hadn't done as she asked. In fact, he'd openly defied Marion's wishes. And he'd done it because in his heroic, Marion-first brain, he'd wanted to take care of her.

Heather was still talking. Her voice faded in and out of Marion's awareness. "We'll have to find Konig quickly...only a few minutes until the wedding, but he had to flee the vote... It sounds like the Raven Knights had to arrest half of the council. I think your doctor friend attacked Konig, so he's probably been arrested too..."

Marion seriously doubted that anyone would have managed to seize Seth. She was surprised he hadn't already materialized to abduct her before she could marry Konig.

The idea wasn't as unappealing as it should have been.

Stupid, selfish Marion.

"You're being called, Your Highness." Her hairstylist grabbed something off of the vanity and offered it to Marion. The white soapstone statuette that Marion and Nori used to communicate with one another was glowing.

"Thank you." Marion gripped it in one hand.

The line of communication activated as soon as her fingers closed around it.

Flashes of words and images cascaded over her. They would have made no sense to anyone who didn't have angel blood—not exactly like a phone call, but more like sharing a moment of perfect unity.

Nori was on the floor of Myrkheimr's throne room.

She was bleeding.

Rearing over Nori was Konig—with an arm locked around his throat and a demon sword near his ribs. Arawn was holding him. And that meant Arawn had done the impossible. Despite relocating the wedding to somewhere sunnier, Arawn was at their wedding.

The sensations ended abruptly.

Marion leaped to her feet with a shriek of shock. "Nori!" Her sudden motion upset the stylists, the stool she'd been sitting on, the table.

Heather had her bow drawn in an instant. "What is it?"

"I need to get to the throne room," Marion

said. "Right now!"

But before she could grab the archer, screaming erupted from outside the windows.

Marion bolted to the window. She already knew what she would see, but infernal power rippling in the shadows between columns was chilling nonetheless. It coursed over the crowd of humans who had been taking their seats for the wedding. Anyone who wasn't sitting in daylight.

"Impossible," Marion whispered, even though she'd already seen Arawn, so she knew it was tragically possible.

That was the only word that she could get out before the entire wing of Myrkheimr collapsed.

It folded like a house of cards, the columns bowing in among themselves, the roof sinking, the floor rising to meet it.

Heather swore loudly and launched out the window, nocking an arrow so quickly that Marion hadn't even seen it come from the quiver.

The archer disappeared into the crowd of fleeing attendees.

"Heather!" Marion shouted, to no response. "Damnation above and below..."

The crowd surged, turning against itself. She tasted the copper tang of blood on the air. Crimson runes raced across the courtyard, crawled up the walls, and ringed the collapsed area.

With a discordant *crash*, hellish energy struck Myrkheimr like a bolt of lightning. Smoke and sulfur poured from dozens of people.

They'd been possessed by demons.

"They collapsed the building so Arawn could invade," Marion breathed.

But how? They shouldn't have been capable of getting a foothold in the Autumn Court at all. That was why they'd moved the wedding from the Winter Court, after all. It was meant to be safer, dammit.

The Raven Knights were closing in on the collapsed wing. It was the most obvious threat, and it would keep everyone occupied while Arawn murdered the soon-to-be King of the Winter Court.

"I'm coming, Nori," Marion said.

Wedding dresses weren't meant for running in. She was cursedly slow, dragging that train behind her, but incapable of getting out of the dress without help. She hitched the skirts as high as she could and pretended not to hear threads popping and diamonds scattering across the floor.

The hallways were flooded with people running—some haloed in auras of infernal power, others bloody from the attack. They were all going the wrong way. Marion had to fight against the tide to head for the throne room.

Marion was three steps from the corner to the next hallway when she tasted that copper tang again and the walls shivered around her.

Dust blasted from around the corner.

The path she'd been about to take had collapsed.

Infernal runes raced from the destruction,

lancing toward her toes. They leaped with the same muted balefire that had guarded Duat in Sheol.

If that stuff touched Marion, she would never stop burning.

She took a page out of Heather's book and leaped through the nearest window.

For a weightless moment, she thought she'd escaped the balefire.

Then she struck the lawn outside, which bordered the western cliffs, and she gagged on smoke. Marion twisted to see that blasted train of her dress on fire. It swarmed through the grass like fireflies that gushed sticky black smoke.

"*Merde!*"

She hacked at her dress with the sharp point of an arrow from her quiver, severing the gauzy train from the rest of the dress. The cloth puddled to the grass, enveloped in fire moments later.

Marion shielded her eyes from the sun and smoke as she gazed up at Myrkheimr.

An explosion thudded through the ground beneath her feet. One of the towers vanished into smoke, collapsing instantly.

She raced for the throne room, taking other paths between the cliffs and waterfalls, running fast enough that the infernal runes couldn't catch up with her. The fight was elsewhere in Myrkheimr—in all the public areas where the wedding had been due to occur. The screaming grew distant as she plunged into the depths of the castle.

She slammed into the throne room.

Konig wasn't there.

Nori was.

Poor, beautiful Nori looked like she'd drowned in her own blood. Angels bled in silver colors, but Nori's human side ran strong. She was drenched in sticky, cherry fluids.

And then Nori gasped.

"Gods!" Marion threw herself beside Nori. For all that she couldn't touch dirty things, she didn't hesitate to press her hands against Nori's wounds, fighting to stem the flow of blood. But it wasn't like there were a few severed vessels. Her whole body was severed. Pinching the skin together didn't help.

She was dying.

Why couldn't Marion summon healing magic to mind?

Nori's unfocused eyes stared in Marion's direction. "Ymir. Konig's magic."

"Shh, don't talk." Marion's fingers trembled while they smoothed over Nori's forehead, smearing blood into her hair. Nori was dying. She deserved to be touched.

It gave no comfort to Nori. Tears slid down her bloodied cheeks. "I'm so sorry, Marion." Her chest jerked. A drop of blood slithered from the corner of her mouth to the corner of her ear. "I never should have—so sorry..."

If she couldn't do magic to save Nori, then Marion should have ended the suffering. It would have been mercy to knock her out, finish the job, whatever it took to save her from drowning in her own blood.

For all her flaws, though, Marion was too similar to Seth in this respect. She couldn't make herself responsible for the moment that Nori's heart stopped beating.

"Hello, Marion."

Her head snapped up.

Arawn stood above her, elbow propped on the back of one throne. A bastard sword dangled casually from his other hand. It was identical to the sword Konig had selected for his duel against Arawn in the Nether Worlds, but this was the weapon that had killed Nori.

"Do you want your fiancé?" Arawn asked. "Or should I just kill the lying dickweed for you right now?"

TWENTY-ONE

The Raven Knights had attempted to arrest Seth. At least, that was what he assumed they'd been trying to do. He hadn't stuck around to see what the royal guard wanted from him.

He'd tried to chase Konig into the throne room and failed. The wards were too strong.

Seth had been trained to hunt werewolves by the best. They were different beasts than faeries, but hunting such powerful creatures was the same in philosophy.

If he couldn't get in the monster's den, he could set a trap.

He went to the courtyard, where the wedding was meant to be held, and he waited.

Seth positioned himself on the balcony overlooking the altar. What he planned to do when Konig showed up—he honestly hadn't thought that far, but he suspected it would be the kind of thing a man didn't walk away from whole, or without regrets.

Konig didn't show up.

Neither did the rest of the wedding party.

"What are you doing?" Rylie approached, trailed by a young teenager who strongly resembled Abel. Not so much around the eyes—those were Rylie's eyes—but in the stubborn set of his jaw, and the sullen way he wore his tuxedo. He looked as though he'd have much preferred a t-shirt and jeans.

"I don't know," Seth said, glaring at the altar. "I'll figure it out by the time Konig shows up."

"Bad blood there, huh?" Rylie asked.

"You have no idea."

The angel who had agreed to perform the ceremony, Jibril, was waiting for the wedding party too. He stood alone on the altar in front of the enormous group of spectators, outwardly serene even though he must have been getting worried.

Everything was ready for the royal wedding except the couple due to get married.

"Do you want to talk about what happened with the vote?" Rylie asked.

Seth forced himself to focus on the Alpha. She was beautiful in that moment, as she was in all moments. She wore a sleek dress befitting her station. Even in her mature clothes, with her lined face, Seth could see the girl he'd fallen in love with.

"Konig's not a good man," Seth said.

"You told me that about Abel once or twice."

"This is different." Konig was a thousand times worse than Abel. A million times worse. Some number that mortal minds couldn't even comprehend.

Rylie hesitated, and then said, "I have something you might want." She led Seth a few feet away from her teenage son and pulled something out of her purse. It was a magazine for a Beretta 9mm. "I assume you're carrying the same gun you always have."

"You assume right." Seth thumbed one of the bullets out. It was iron—a metal that could kill the sidhe. He turned shocked eyes on Rylie.

"I don't get searched," she said. "You seemed worried about events with Marion, and I just thought..." Rylie trailed off, as though unsure how to justify carrying a deadly weapon in her purse.

"Thank you," Seth said. He pocketed the magazine. "Seriously. Thanks."

"Did I introduce you to my son, Benjamin?" Rylie asked lightly. "Benjamin, this is Seth Wilder."

The teenage boy's eyes widened. "Wilder?"

"Seth is your uncle," she said. "You might have heard your older siblings talk about him before."

"Wow," Benjamin said.

Seth shook hands with Benjamin Gresham—or perhaps Benjamin Wilder. He wasn't sure. He didn't want to ask. Like Marion had pointed out, Rylie and Abel had never married.

"You look young to be my uncle," Benjamin said. The fact that he was remarking on age rather than the exposed organs was telling. This was a boy who had grown up with Alphas, and very little surprised him.

Seth didn't want to explain that he was a god who had once been engaged to his mother. He settled for saying, "It's nice to finally meet you."

Benjamin probably planned to keep talking, but that was when people started screaming.

A rumble spread through Myrkheimr, followed by crashing.

Seth had a moment to register the dust that spilled from a crack in the mezzanine's roof before it collapsed.

He dived.

If he were asked later, he'd have said that he was going for Rylie. But it wasn't Rylie who he wrapped his arms around. It was Benjamin, teenage son of Abel Wilder.

Seth's momentum carried both of them well out of the range of rubble. They struck the ground within the courtyard.

Benjamin came up gasping, his hair whitened by rubble. "Mom."

Seth's mortal ears were ringing. His core ached from his spine to the place his abdominals should have been, and the world swam around him.

Part of Myrkheimr had collapsed. Kindred energy sang to him from the resulting shadows, and infernal magic flowed through the crowd.

Possessed.

Seth could feel that in his core as surely as he felt his heart beating.

Dozens—hundreds—of the human attendees to Marion and Konig's wedding had been seized by demon energy in that same heartbeat that an entire wing of Myrkheimr collapsed.

He was surrounded by chunks of rubble large enough that they easily could have crushed people into glue. Had Seth been anyone else, he doubted he'd have ever walked again. But many injured victims were standing. They were walking. Some were even running.

That was the demon force seizing them.

Chaos spread through the crowd.

What had been an orderly crowd barely minutes earlier had turned into a churning mass of bodies. There were no fire codes in the Middle Worlds and no laws about safe crowd capacities; likewise, there were no emergency exits that would ensure people could escape such situations safely.

Bodies smashed into Seth. He was squeezed tight, carried against a pillar as people struggled to escape. Feet smashed his feet. Elbows pummeled his ribs. The crowd grew so tight that he could barely turn his head.

When he looked down, he saw a face pressed to his knees. An adult man. Someone who had fallen and was wailing as he struggled to escape. The crowd had gone wild so quickly that there was simply nowhere to go.

Damn. Those who were possessed by demons

didn't need to rip people apart like they had in Rock Bottom. Everyone was getting trampled underfoot, pressed against columns, buried under rubble.

Seth had never heard screaming so horrible before.

And he didn't see Rylie anywhere.

"Hold your breath!" he shouted, shoving his hand between two strangers to grab Benjamin's shoulder.

Seth snapped his fingers.

With a whirlwind of brimstone, he vanished from the crush of the crowd in the courtyard.

There was an instant—less than the span of time it took him to inhale—that he stepped through Sheol with Rylie's son, his nephew, cradled in his arms like a very tall infant.

Then he reappeared atop a part of Myrkheimr that had yet to fall apart. It was more horrifying to see everything from that perspective. It gave Seth a high-level view of the devastation, which meant he didn't see many of the wounds, the splatters of blood, the faces slack in death. But he saw bodies falling. He saw people writhing under rubble. He saw the swarm of demons within the shadow.

No Rylie.

No *Marion*.

Seth set Benjamin down. "Are you okay?"

"Yeah, I'm fine." He brushed himself off. "Where's my mom?"

It was a great question, but Rylie would never forgive Seth if he took one of her sons into danger.

He phased Benjamin outside of the castle and deposited him on flat ground.

"Stay here," Seth said firmly.

Benjamin was disoriented by multiple jumps through the Autumn Court. His eyes could barely focus. "What?"

Seth phased again.

He returned to what had been the mezzanine moments earlier. There was no sign of Rylie among all the broken stone fragments.

Seth phased again, and again, and again, trying to find her.

When he reappeared on a flat patch of ground underneath columns that had fallen together, like the poles of a tent, he found humans with glowing eyes and infernal runes swirling over their foreheads. People possessed by demons.

But still no Rylie.

The demons reacted to Seth's appearance by lurching toward him. Seth could taste the Nether Worlds on the air that they exhaled. Shredded souls clung to them—the aftermath of all the murders they'd committed. These were Arawn's creatures, no doubt about it. The Lord of Sheol was getting the revenge he wanted.

"Stop," Seth said.

Energy filled that one word. Seth hadn't even known he had that kind of energy within him. Something so powerful, so *fatal*, that the demon-possessed wedding attendees in their dresses and tuxedos couldn't help but obey.

They froze where they stood, staring at him.

Seth reached his senses along the cables of infernal power to feel for its origin. It was no surprise that Arawn was holding the puppet strings. What surprised him was the nearness of the demon.

Arawn was in the Autumn Court.

"Wait there," Seth said, pointing at the possessed ones so they would understand.

He leaped into the courtyard again.

The survivors who had been capable of escaping had cleared out at that point, leaving behind dozens of crushed, motionless dead. There was enough space to breathe, and enough space to see possessed ones swarming in the shadows. He also saw Rylie on the ground near the altar, lying in the one beam of sunlight that could shine through the shattered castle. Someone must have dragged her there for safety's sake, but her guards were nowhere in sight.

That shapeshifter from the American Gaean Commission, Deirdre Tombs, was standing over her. Just like Seth remembered from her moments of death.

Seth drew his guns.

Neither Deirdre nor Rylie noticed his approach. There was no world outside of the two of them, their golden eyes connected in that sunbeam, safe from Arawn's followers.

Some part of Seth was horrified by how easily he aimed both barrels at Deirdre Tombs's s skull.

His fingers tensed.

But then he realized Deirdre's motions weren't

aggressive. She was reaching toward Rylie, gripping the Alpha's hand, and helping her stand. Even as Rylie got up on wobbling legs, Seth could see that the wounds inflicted by Myrkheimr's collapse were healing. Rylie's cuts and bruises faded to nothing, leaving no sign of what had happened aside from smears of blood.

Deirdre was going to kill Rylie someday.

Not *that* day.

Seth jammed a gun back into his belt, freeing an arm to grab the Alpha. Rylie fell against him.

"Benjamin," she said.

"Safe," Seth replied.

The relief in Rylie's expression was familiar. It had been decades since she'd looked at him like that, but it felt like no time had passed at all. The timelessness of godhood took on new meaning.

But then she said, "Marion."

He shocked back to the present.

Marion.

Where was she?

Seth's eyes swept the area. He didn't see a hint of her—not so much as a flash of Winter Court white.

While he'd been distracted with Rylie, he had forgotten his intent to protect the bride-to-be. And he hadn't seen her anywhere.

Rylie pushed away from him, grabbing Deirdre Tombs for support as though they trusted one another as much as Seth and Rylie. "Do what you have to do," Deirdre said, fixing Seth with her fierce hawk eyes. "I've got Rylie."

He couldn't trust her. Dammit, he knew for a *fact* that Deirdre was going to shoot Rylie right between the eyebrows.

Rylie knew that too, but she still had an arm looped over Deirdre's shoulders as she healed.

"Take care of her," Rylie said.

That was the last encouragement he needed.

He phased.

Arawn had been unsettling to encounter in the depths of the Nether Worlds. Amid the rustic beauty of the Autumn Court, he was downright terrifying.

He wore leather in shades of pink that suggested it had been tanned from no animal. The vest swooped low in the front to expose a skeletal chest not unlike Seth's, and chains connected his studded collar to his wrists. A domino mask made of scorched iron and barbed wire concealed half of his face. Horrible yet formal.

It seemed that he had dressed up for her wedding.

Marion stood, dress heavy with Nori's blood. "What have you done?"

"Come and see," Arawn said, sweeping a hand toward the door behind the throne room.

Marion went to see.

She only took one step into the chamber behind the throne room before she lost the strength to keep moving.

Arawn had brought Hell into the Autumn Court.

What had once been a room for entertaining political guests had been cast in total shadow, its windows bricked, the witchlights replaced with lanterns fueled by bowls of fat. Kennels were positioned around the walls. The white-furred Hounds from Marion's nightmares snarled inside, barely contained by flimsy bars.

In the middle of it all was the King of the Autumn Court, Rage. He had been chained to the wall and flayed.

He'd clearly been there for a long time. Weeks, maybe. Effluence caked his leather pants. There were plates discarded around him. A bucket that smelled like urine, even at that distance.

No wonder Rage hadn't been participating in wedding preparations.

Konig was limp in a puddle of faerie limbs beside him. Arawn had lost his first duel against Konig, so he'd come prepared for the second duel. And Konig had clearly lost. He was unconscious.

Arawn strolled along the edge of the room, his sword carving a line in the floor. "You've got questions and I've got answers. Why did Leliel attack Niflheimr? She didn't. Why did Konig lie about that? Because he didn't want you to know what Charity saw. And where is Charity, you ask? She's in the Nether Worlds with me, and you can't have her back."

"What did Charity see?" Marion asked.

"She saw me, for one," Arawn said. "For another, she saw your fiancé making out with your cousin. From the sounds of it, Konig and Nori were sharing one hell of an embrace."

The magic Marion had struggled to summon for Nori began to flow through her, fed by hatred. "You're a demon. Why should I believe anything you say?"

"I don't really care if you do," Arawn said. "I like watching you undergo a little soul-searching. I wish you'd done more soul-searching before shattering the gods-damned Canope and ruining my deal with the gods." He sighed. "Too little, too late."

He rested the point of the sword on Konig's breastbone.

Marion thrust a hand toward Arawn, letting the magic of her anger pour from her palm.

It sputtered. Flickered. Barely lit the room.

Arawn looked disappointed that Marion hadn't hurt him. "Why aren't you blasting me into nothingness? It's not that you still don't remember your magic, is it? Gosh, that wouldn't be a problem if you *hadn't broken the Canope*."

Marion lifted the bow over her head. She had an arrow aimed at Arawn in a heartbeat. Heather wasn't the only lightning-fast archer in Myrkheimr, and Marion didn't need magic to be deadly. "Step away from Konig."

To her surprise, Arawn slunk toward her. "Do you know what an ascension is?"

"It's when demons gather power to rise in the

hierarchy," she said, adjusting her stance so she could track Arawn with the arrow. "It's why you're killing everyone and burning their souls in the Pit."

"Ascensions haven't worked since Genesis. The gods saw fit to get rid of them. Thought the system could be exploited, I bet. Can't imagine why." The corner of Arawn's lips tugged into a smirk. "I've been burning the souls in the Pit because I want Seth's attention. I want him to be God. Only he can give me what I want."

"Sunlight," Marion said faintly.

"Sunlight," Arawn agreed.

His attack on the wedding was an ascension—but not for Arawn.

Marion released the arrow.

It seemed to appear in Arawn's throat by magic, in much the same way that Seth could teleport between planes.

There was no blood. Arawn's mouth opened wide, exposing rows upon rows of jagged teeth. The seam of his lips tore down his neck. The arrow simply fell out and his mouth kept opening.

Gods, he was just as bad as his Hounds.

Marion flung herself away from the doors, nocking another arrow. She whispered a basic incantation of fire and ice as she pulled the string back to her cheek.

The second arrow punched into the back of his throat. It exploded. He stumbled, mouth contracting.

Marion threw herself to Konig and tugged at

the chains, seeking the lock.

He stirred. "Get out of here, princess..."

"Shut up." Marion squeezed her hands over the shackle. "Open, damn you!" Magic zapped. Locks clicked. The metal fell open, tumbling away from his skin to reveal angry red welts. Arawn had chained Konig with iron: a metal as deadly to the sidhe as silver was to wolves.

She kicked the shackles away from him. Getting them out of his reach was like turning a light on in his brain. His eyes widened and he sat upright, as strong as when she'd last seen him.

"Arawn," Konig snarled.

The prince thrust his hand into the air, summoning the six-foot bastard sword that was his preferred weapon. It arrived in the throne room with the sound of chimes and a shower of amber light. He gripped it in both hands.

The hoarse howl of a dog made Marion turn.

Arawn had his head thrown back, screeching like a Hound going on the hunt. The veins in his throat and arms bulged.

Then he leaped.

Konig shoved Marion aside, putting himself in Arawn's path. He thrust the blade into Arawn's mouth.

It sank into the roof of his impossibly massive mouth with a gush of black ichor.

Arawn kicked, sending Konig flying. But before the prince could hit the wall, he flashed back onto his feet, jumping through the ley lines to stand behind Arawn. He had home territory advantage now. And Arawn had lost the element of surprise.

They fought as only a demon and a sidhe could, making the world twist like the eye of a hurricane. It took all of Marion's willpower to focus on loosening Rage's shackles instead of the fight.

With another whip-crack of magic, she released him. The king sagged to the floor.

"Wake up," Marion said, shaking him gently. "You need to wake up. You need to activate the wards against Arawn."

One of his eyes peeled open. "Marion? You have to get out of here, kitten. Arawn...Violet..." He couldn't seem to get what he wanted to say out. He tugged at the collar of his shirt, exposing his chest.

Marion sucked in a gasp.

Rage had been branded with an infernal rune that pulsed with deadly power.

"What does it mean?" Marion asked.

He passed out before he could respond.

Marion stood slowly. The horror that crawled over her was powerful enough that she couldn't breathe. How was it possible she hadn't realized what was happening until that moment? Arawn's demons had gotten a foothold in the Autumn Court because their lord had been there for days —maybe weeks—holding the king hostage.

"Mother!"

The sound of Konig's shout made Marion's head snap up.

The Onyx Queen had entered the room. Her hair was smeared with ash and dust from the collapses elsewhere in the castle.

Konig and Arawn were locked in battle, hilt-to-hilt, magic thrashing around them. "Mother, help!" the prince shouted.

Marion drew another arrow and aimed at the Onyx Queen, dread squeezing her heart.

Violet wasn't going to help Konig because defying Arawn would mean Rage's death by that infernal rune.

The queen pointed at her son. Magic gathered at her fingertip.

Marion released the arrow, and it flew with aim as perfect as when she'd been shooting for Arawn. The point punched into Violet's shoulder.

It wasn't iron, so the queen's arm only dropped. The spell she cast smashed into the floor instead. Tiles exploded a few feet from Konig's feet. "Mother!" he cried. This time, the word was wracked with betrayal. His eyes were wide. "What are you doing?"

Arawn shoved Konig to the ground. "Myrkheimr is mine. The entire Autumn Court is mine, royal family inclusive." When he spoke, his enormous mouth swirled, the teeth twisting in a vortex that threatened to consume everything. "Long live the king."

TWENTY-TWO

Seth had never needed to rapid-fire phase between multiple locations before. He'd spent a decade trying not to use preternatural powers, so on the rare occasions that he had taken advantage, it had been when he desperately needed to get somewhere in particular.

He was desperate now, but he didn't know where to go.

Flash.

He reappeared on the lawn close to where he'd left Rylie's son. Benjamin was still there, a few dozen feet away, helping usher people through the fences demarcating Myrkheimr's lawns from the forest beyond.

Flash.

Marion wasn't in her bedroom.

Flash.

She wasn't in Konig's, either.

Flash.

Seth reappeared in the broken foyer. Raven Knights battled humans who were possessed alongside Rylie's guards, and that one sidhe archer who was always tagging along with Konig —what was her name? Heather? She had access to the restricted throne room.

He grabbed the archer. Heather looked surprised, but there was no chance to explain.

"You're coming with me," he said, holding her wrist tightly.

Flash.

They reappeared outside the throne room. Heather dropped to her knees and vomited in much the same way that Marion usually did.

"Sorry, but we don't have time for you to recover," Seth said.

He hauled Heather off of her feet and wrapped her hand around the handle to the throne room door.

She elbowed him in the gut.

The archer seemed to know just where to aim. The blow went underneath his breastbone and connected with his vulnerable heart. It hurt like nothing else had—not even having Myrkheimr dropped on top of him. It staggered him. He groaned.

The touch of Heather's hand on the door was enough to make it swing open, though. Both of them saw inside simultaneously.

They saw the body in front of the thrones—

Nori's body—and the massive puddle of blood creeping across the tiles.

"Gods above," Heather said.

"That's why I brought you here," Seth said, scrambling to his feet with his arms folded around his aching chest. "Konig—Marion—"

"Understood." She pulled a new arrow out and lifted her bow. "Sorry about the elbow thing."

Marion's cry echoed through the throne room.

There was an open door behind the dais where the king and queen should have been sitting. Her voice came from that direction.

Seth drew his Beretta and exchanged magazines. Iron instead of lead. He wasn't going to let anyone hurt Marion again.

"Follow me," he said. He punched into the next room, guns drawn, with Heather on his left.

In a heartbeat, he saw it all.

The king collapsed against the wall.

The queen with magic thrashing around her fist.

An entire pack of Hounds kenneled under the boarded windows.

Arawn standing over Konig, gaping mouth hanging open to expose the multitude of teeth within his jaw.

And Marion.

She looked a lot like her sister when she was drenched in blood, armed with a bow, and wearing a shredded wedding dress. Seth could easily imagine Marion as a Godslayer. The woman who would bury an arrow deep in his heart and ruin his life.

Violet unleashed a fistful of magic aimed right at Marion.

It didn't seem like that much of a betrayal at this point. Seth had been waiting for this moment ever since the summit, when he'd told Marion that he believed the royal family was out to get her.

Seth didn't need another moment of thought to fire his gun.

And he shot to kill.

A bullet hole appeared in Violet's back. The queen pitched forward. But the deadly magic she had been gathering in her fist had already been released, churning toward Marion in seeming slow motion.

Seth phased.

He wrapped his arms around Marion's waist and phased again.

They reappeared, and her quiver scattered arrows across the floor of the throne room. She was gasping for breath, clawing at her throat, coughing up blood from the briefest exposure to Sheol. The taste of death wasn't as sweet on her as it had been in the past. There were many other souls waiting to be claimed in the Autumn Court, and they called to Seth much louder.

Seth sank to his knees while holding her, watching to make sure she started breathing again.

She did.

"You spoke out against Konig," Marion gasped. It seemed a ridiculous thing to be focused on during a total assault against Myrkheimr.

To be fair, it was also at the forefront of Seth's mind.

"I'd do it again," he said.

She got up, hand pressed to her chest. It must have been difficult to breathe in the restrictive wedding dress, but she still found the strength to stand tall and look Seth in the eye. "Thank you for taking care of me."

The wall behind the thrones exploded.

Arawn erupted through the rubble, clutching Heather's hair in one fist, and Konig's hair in the other. The archer was alive but unconscious; the prince was conscious but not fighting. Seth knew that look of shock. It had been on Abel's face when their mother had been killed.

Violet was dead.

"Took you long enough to get here, Seth," Arawn said. He tossed both Konig and Heather aside. "I thought I was going to have to skin Marion to get your attention at this rate."

"You know that I am what you only pretend to be," Seth said. "So you know how serious I am when I tell you not to touch Marion."

"Do you really think a human avatar can stand up against a Lord of Sheol at the height of his powers?" Arawn tossed Konig aside with a laugh. "Let's find out!"

Another explosion shook the room. Cracks raced up the walls. The roof beams sagged, and then snapped. The roof began to fall.

Marion and Seth leaped at the same time. But

where Seth tried to grab Marion to phase out of the throne room, Marion went for Nori's body. "Save her!" she cried.

It was too late. Nori was dead, soul severed from her physical body. Seth could tell because he thirsted to consume her death. Marion didn't realize, and she bowed over the body while the roof fell around them.

The only thing Seth could do was shield Marion from the worst of the rubble. It struck his back. He barely felt it.

Marion was touching Nori's throat, feeling for a pulse. The horror of truth dawned in her eyes. "No."

"I'm sorry," he said. "I'm so sorry."

"Boo," Arawn said. He'd appeared on the other side of Nori's body while they were distracted. He wrapped an arm around Marion's throat, yanking her off of her feet.

Crimson runes raced in a circle around them, erupting with a flash so bright that Seth's night vision was instantly wrecked. It formed a towering dome of smokeless flame that sheared the rubble apart where it touched.

Balefire.

They were trapped inside the circle with Arawn.

Seth was standing, aiming his gun at the demon's leering face, and he hadn't even felt himself move. He didn't shoot. The iron bullets would do nothing to Arawn, and he was holding Marion in front of him like a shield anyway.

"Think of this," Arawn purred in her ear, "if you'd just taken your memories, then I wouldn't have had to fight for my freedom. Every single soul that's burned in balefire is your fault."

"Nobody is responsible for the evil you've done except you," Seth said. "Blame it on the victims if you want, but we all know who's culpable."

"How much does culpability matter, in the end? The result is the same." Arawn scraped one of his fingers down the side of Marion's throat. He was wearing a metal claw over his nail, and it left a crimson line on her delicate flesh. "Let your mortal form die so you can ascend. I won't kill Marion if you give me immunity to sunlight as soon as you cross over."

"I've got another deal for you," Marion hissed at him over her shoulder. "Let me go and I won't emasculate you."

"Petty threats," Arawn began to say.

Marion punched her fist backward.

She was holding one of her arrows. She buried the point in between Arawn's legs, driving it into the place where humans kept their manhood.

Apparently Lords of Sheol were assembled in a similar fashion.

He released her with a shriek. Ichor spurted over his leather pants.

Seth ripped Marion away from Arawn, into the relative safety of his arms—but that was as far as they could go. Balefire wouldn't let them pass through it without burning. According to Dana, they couldn't phase through, either.

There was only one way that they were going to get out of this.

Seth gripped Marion by the back of her neck. Pressed their foreheads together. "Read my mind. *Please*."

This time, he felt Marion inside his skull.

He focused his thoughts on his memories of godhood—how detached he'd been while omnipotent, how little he'd cared when he had seen Rylie's death, how it hurt him to be distant like that.

It was an apology he couldn't bring himself to speak aloud, not when he wouldn't be able to explain it well enough.

Marion looked horrified. "Don't go. Please don't go."

He'd have given her anything else she asked for.

It was sheer impulse—base animal instinct, the craving for touch—that made him brush his lips over her cheek, like when he'd kissed her forehead after the summit. A gesture he could convince himself was fraternal, friendly, platonic.

She turned her head at the last moment and lips brushed against lips, just a little bit, the barest touch. Her breath tasted of smoked wood. It whispered over his mouth and then she inhaled, tasting him.

Her lips were so soft. A man could have lost himself in that touch.

Seth pushed Marion behind him.

He threw himself at Arawn.

Both Seth and Arawn plunged through the wall of balefire.

The instantaneous incineration of Seth's body didn't even hurt. It happened too quickly.

His avatar was gone.

Seth remained oriented to mortal time in the moments that followed, even as his consciousness slipped sideways into a more god-like state.

In those moments, he remembered he had killed himself to end the fight with Arawn. So he ended it.

Even he couldn't destroy balefire easily, so he relocated the flames to Duat, allowing it to meld with the rest of its ilk.

The throne room was safe.

Nori's soul hovered over her body, floating unseen beside Marion. The half-angel mage was increasingly disinteresting to Seth. She had years of life ahead of her. She wasn't his business like Nori was.

No. Not disinteresting. Not Marion. Focus—don't forget.

He had to do his job.

Seth reached out by instinct, seizing the ephemeral glow of Nori's spirit. He saw her as an apparition of herself: a petite, semi-transparent woman with no hair or clothes. The ghost of the half-angel who had been. "There's a door," Nori's spirit said. There was nothing audible about her voice. Marion wouldn't be able to hear it.

Seth's heart twisted. "I know. Go toward the door, Nori." His response was equally silent.

Hundreds more souls were scattered throughout the Autumn Court, their souls yearning away from the bodies that contained them.

Seth couldn't do anything for the ones Arawn had already burned, but he could still save the others.

He reached out with the entirety of his being and scooped all those other souls into his arms. The throne room warped around them as Seth followed Nori into the Nether.

Arawn was right behind Seth. He'd died in the balefire too, but death seemed to be a different thing for the Lords of Sheol. Nyx had lingered after being murdered, and so did Arawn. "You're killing them all," Arawn taunted. "It's all your fault."

"No," Seth said. "It's yours."

Taking responsibility for people killed by Arawn would have been like Marion taking responsibility for Konig's actions.

It was *wrong*.

The Pit of Souls was burning with Arawn's balefire when Seth arrived with the victims from Myrkheimr. He pulled the balefire away with a thought as brief as the one that had stripped it from the throne room. Now Duat's flaming shield was miles thick. It touched the edge of the Dead Forest. So much balefire for one little Nether World.

Hundreds of souls hung over his shoulders, heavier than a cloak of lead. He still clasped hands with Nori's blank-eyed apparition.

They were ready to go through the door.

"Come with us," Seth said, reaching out for Arawn.

The demon's spirit hovered a few feet away, his braids lashing behind him in the wind generated by balefire. "Think it through. You don't want me to die."

Seth heard him, but he didn't really care about the question. Arawn was dead. He needed to send him where he belonged in the Pit of Souls so that he could be disassembled, remixed, and spit out as new life.

But wasn't there something he still needed from Arawn?

"Charity," Seth said. "Where's Charity?"

"I can tell you she's not in Duat anymore, and she won't survive if you kill me," Arawn said. "Let me go. I'll find a new body. I'll take care of Charity."

Seth didn't know if that was the right thing to do. He couldn't tell anymore.

He only knew that it was time to go.

Slowly, over the span of eternity, he turned toward the Pit of Souls with the charges who needed him. Nothing remained in the chasm after that except vast, empty *nothing*, where souls could sink and sink, waiting for the instant of rebirth. He released them all at once.

Everyone but Arawn.

And then Seth followed them down.

Marion's last cry was still trailing him.

Please don't go.

He still cared for one moment.

What was a moment in the span of a god's experience, though? Was it a heartbeat, or the entirety of eternity that stretched between one Genesis and the next?

The caring drained out of him as he continued to sink.

Seth remembered the things he'd forgotten when substantiating. Every single detail of his eons ruling Sheol with Nyx. The instant that the Genesis void had consumed all of the planet.

Even an eternity coexisting with Elise and James.

Becoming the third god to a couple like them —a pair who were madly in love, with an emphasis on the "mad"—was worse than being a third wheel. He had been a roommate for two people who hadn't cared about anyone else. But their room had been an entire universe, and Seth had been incapable of getting away.

Worse, they hadn't wanted him to get away. They'd wanted him to suffer. They'd wanted him to be Death.

"I made you and you'll do what I tell you," Elise had said at one point. "If I want you to perform surgery on yourself, you'll do it. If I want you to hop on one foot while barking like a dog for a thousand years, you'll do it. And if I want you to kill my sister—"

"Just because you made me doesn't mean you own me," Seth had said.

And Elise had said, "You'll regret saying that."

She'd been right.

Seth's only option to escape Elise and James had been to flee to a place gods didn't care about: mortality.

Gods didn't care about mortals.

Seth didn't care about mortals.

The souls were taken by the Pit, and he felt a distant, momentary satisfaction over a job well done.

Then he felt nothing.

TWENTY-THREE

It was quiet after Seth and Arawn left. All Marion could hear was a soft weeping. She needed a few minutes to realize that the weeping was coming from her.

She got up, swiping the tears off of her cheeks. She didn't have time to mourn for Nori's empty body in a puddle of blood. She didn't even have time to mourn losing Seth.

Marion stumbled over the rubble to get to Konig. He was waking up. She helped him to his feet. "He shot my mom," Konig said, his voice raw. "Seth killed my mother."

"He was trying to protect me," Marion said.

"You don't understand. Seth killed the Queen of the Autumn Court and control is matrilineal. You've seen what happened to Niflheimr when its queen died." Its protective magic had unraveled and the court had become a wasteland.

"But Rage—"

"Matrilineal," he snapped. "He's not king without a queen." Konig pressed both hands to his temples, eyes squeezing shut. "The wards are already breaking down."

Footsteps thudded among the rubble. Rocks slipped and shifted.

Hounds emerged from the chamber behind the thrones, loosed from the kennels that had contained them. Violet wasn't the only ruler who had died. Seth had taken out Arawn, and there was nobody to hold the Hounds anymore.

One of them lunged for Heather Cobweb's unconscious body.

Konig swept her off of the ground before it could bite, leaping backwards. Its mouth snapped on the heel of his boot. Sidhe blood spattered the floor.

Marion lifted her bow, heart pounding. Her arrows would do nothing against the Hounds.

A loud crash.

The collapsed rubble exploded. Jibril punched his way through it, landing between Marion and Konig with his wings flared. Even in the midst of so much destruction, the angel was clean and composed. "What in the names of the gods happened here?"

"My mother's dead," Konig said.

Jibril understood without the explanation Marion had needed. "Then there's only one thing to do."

He grabbed both Konig and Marion and burst into flight.

They lifted from the throne room, leaving the Hounds among the wreckage. Only when they were in the air did Marion realize exactly how far they were from the rest of Myrkheimr. The enchanted throne room was on a cliff in the depths of the forest, overlooking the rest of the kingdom.

From there, Marion could see the white shapes of the Hounds pouring through the trees, racing for the burning castle.

A dozen Hounds would do a lot of damage to the wedding attendees.

Jibril landed on one of the few towers that were still standing. There was an altar at its top, much like the kind that Marion had in the Winter Court. It must have been one of the points where the soul-linked wards could be connected with blood.

"You know what needs to happen," Jibril said. "You both know."

Marion's heart sank into her stomach.

And it kept sinking.

It sank and sank and sank like balefire eating its way through the Earth's mantle, heading straight for the burning liquid core.

"We have to get married," she said.

Because the queen was dead, the wards had failed, and the Hounds were about to kill everyone —not just the innocents of the Autumn Court, but the members of the council who had been attending Marion's wedding. The leaders of every preternatural organization in the world.

If the Hounds killed them, then all of the world would be thrown into chaos.

"We have to get married as quickly as possible," Marion reiterated, and it was a struggle to get the words out when her whole body was shaking. "Then Konig can fix everything. He can save the Autumn Court."

Grim realization crept over Konig. "I'll be king of both unseelie courts." He seemed to take no pleasure in the knowledge.

"Take one another's hands," Jibril said.

Konig grabbed Marion's wrists since her hands were limp. "Skip the ceremony. Just do the important parts."

Jibril put his hands over theirs. He focused on the prince first. "Do you consent to marriage with Marion Garin, and swear to love, honor, and obey her until death parts you?"

Sidhe magic flared over Konig's flesh, sparking throughout the crystalline walls of Myrkheimr. The oath was not merely words.

"I will love, honor, and obey you, Marion," Konig said.

It felt like chains were looped around Marion's throat, tightening with every syllable.

Myrkheimr shook. Smoke billowed up the

sides of the tower, spreading black clouds into a perfect blue sky. All of the Autumn Court was falling into darkness.

Jibril was calm as he turned his focus on Marion. "Do you consent to marriage with Prince ErlKonig, and swear to love, honor, and obey him until death parts you?"

Magic flashed again. In the glint of light, Marion remembered being struck by Konig. She remembered the fear. The pain.

She remembered Seth's promise to never hurt her.

And then Seth plunging into balefire with Arawn.

"You have to consent," Jibril said. "You have to say the words."

Marion blinked, and the tears started flowing down her cheeks. They dripped from her chin and splattered on the chest of her torn wedding dress. "I will love, honor, and obey you, Konig," she said hoarsely.

The magic yanked tight.

Under calmer circumstances, it would have been a beautiful thing—the way that it wound around them like loops of spider webbing, joining their hearts and bodies.

Marion and Konig joined eternally in holy matrimony.

It was Konig's moment of triumph, but he looked every inch as ragged as Marion. It might have been delusion that led her to think that he looked regretful.

"Hold me," Konig said. "Don't let go."

She continued to grip one of his hands while he extended the other toward Jibril.

The angel slashed his palm.

Blood the color of silver-edged sapphires gushed from Konig's flesh. And then there was no flesh at all. There was only the power at Konig's core. Reality's loose grip unraveled to reveal the truth of him—the sidhe rather than the man she'd married.

Marion had seen him like that before, when he'd been trying to rescue her in Port Angeles. He was raw Earth energy. He was the wind that carried in the first storms of winter. He was the thunderstorm, the hurricane, the tornado carving valleys into planes and flattening every human habitation in its way.

Konig was magic.

He was Myrkheimr.

The wave of the new king's power crested over the Autumn Court, carrying Marion's consciousness along with it. She could see every inch of his kingdom—*their* kingdom. She saw fires extinguished in a heartbeat. Walls lifted from victims trapped within the wreckage. Hounds ripped apart and flung into the ocean.

Konig's presence was so mighty that he consumed Marion's senses. She was only half-human, but half was enough.

He overwhelmed her. All sense of the world shut down.

And then Marion awoke, lying on her back at

the center of the tower. There was no howling, no screaming, no magic. She sat up, her hair frizzed into a foam around her head, with no sign of the pins that had carefully held it in place.

Konig braced himself on the altar, back in his man-like form. He shined brighter than the moon. His eyes radiated. He had taken over the wards on Myrkheimr and driven out all invaders—not just the Hounds, but the possessed human beings, too.

Nothing remained in their kingdom but silence.

There was very little to recover in the wake of the wedding.

At another time, Marion would have been impressed by how effortlessly Konig's magic reassembled the Autumn Court. Myrkheimr didn't seem to require reconstruction, but simple healing; within minutes, it was restored to the same state as the day before without so much as a bloody Hound paw print marring its halls.

Fixing Myrkheimr didn't bring back the dead.

Marion and Konig agreed to make their first appearance as king and queen barely an hour later. It was just enough time for Marion to strip off the bloody wedding dress in numb silence. The diadem that Violet had commissioned was in a box on her dresser, but Marion didn't put it on.

She attended the mass funeral with her hair

loose around her shoulders and wearing the one black dress she'd found in her closet. It must have been designed for another funeral. That was the only occasion Marion could imagine warranting such a modest gown.

Konig was stiff beside her as all the bodies were laid out in the courtyard.

Two hundred thirty-six in all, counting Violet and Nori.

In the wake of battle, the ruling king and queen were meant to spend a night holding vigil over the people they'd lost. Marion doubted that the vigil had been held by freshly coronated newlyweds before, but then, the sidhe hadn't had very long to practice their traditions.

"We don't have to do this," Marion said. "We can have them buried immediately."

"It's sidhe tradition," Konig replied dully.

She didn't offer to end the vigil early again.

They didn't sit, didn't move, and barely spoke as hours passed. They should have been celebrating their wedding night. All of the sidhe courts should have launched into weeks of partying.

Instead, they waited with the dead.

It wasn't his mother's body that he lingered over as the evening wore on, but Nori's. Her body was cast in shades of crimson and amber from the sunset, which made the smears of blood on her body look black.

"Arawn said you were having an affair with her," Marion said. She wasn't sure if she hoped he'd deny it or not. At that point, it seemed like cheating on her was one of the less damaging things he could have done.

He didn't deny anything.

"I need sex the way you need to breathe, princess. Should I have suffocated while waiting for you? Or should I have forced myself on you? I chose to fulfill my own sexual needs so you'd have room to rediscover yourself. What would you have preferred I do?"

"There had to be better options than that," Marion said.

"Don't pretend you're innocent." He sounded as emotionless as she felt. "Don't pretend any of this wouldn't have happened if you weren't falling in love with one of your gods."

"Ymir saw everything, didn't he?" Marion asked. "That's why he's not talking. You did that to him."

"Yes, a hex," Konig said.

That made her angrier than learning he'd slept with Nori.

Marion walked away from him to try to compose herself. She didn't go far—only to the fresh growth of vines against one pillar, where she could inhale the scent of its pollen and stroke her fingers over the soft leaves.

Once they left the courtyard, the surviving members of the Autumn Court would come in to pay their respects, the bodies would be buried, and there would be other matters of state to address. This might have been Marion's only opportunity to talk everything over with Konig for weeks to come.

"We can't divorce," he called to her.

She had already been inching toward that thought, trying to avoid drawing the same conclusion. "It exhausts me, the thought of staying with you. I'll worry you're hexing people to hide information from me. Or I'll worry you'll throw yourself at Heather if I withhold sex one night. Or worry that you'll be enraged by some perceived insult and take it out on me, physically or magically. It is *exhausting*."

Those words didn't evoke fresh anger from him. When he looked beaten like this, it was difficult to imagine that Konig could ever have become angry enough to hit her. "I've made mistakes."

So had Marion. Her entire life had become an attempt to rectify the errors she'd made before losing her memories, and the errors he'd made in the weeks since. "Are you sorry?"

He nodded as he stared at Nori's face. "I've never been sorrier for anything. I'd do better by you, if you let me."

"I don't know why I should."

"If not for me, then for our people. We rule all of the unseelie now, Marion. I just don't think I can do it without you."

"I won't be able to trust you ever again," Marion said. "How can we rule together when we can't win the war between ourselves?"

"Because we need to." He stepped between the

bodies to join Marion, gripping her hand the way that he had when they'd exchanged vows. "You deserve better than me, but I need you now more than ever. Thousands of people need you."

She didn't respond.

Yet the silence from the dead was deeper.

Marion could punish Konig by leaving him—and what a satisfying punishment that would be. The easiest thing to do, by far.

All of the unseelie would suffer for it.

"I'll stay with you," she said. Konig leaned in to kiss her, but she pulled back before he could. "We'll rule together, but I do this for the people, not for you. I want to love you, Konig, but until you prove that you can do better, I'm not going to be with you...like that."

Some of that familiar old anger flickered in his eyes. "You'll want me to remain chaste too, won't you?"

"If you want to salvage our marriage," she said. "Yes. You'll be chaste. You'll *suffocate*. And you'll be happy I've given you the opportunity." Gods, that was a cruel thing to say. It hurt to say it. It was the sweetest pain she'd ever felt.

"I'll wait for you if you'll wait for me," Konig said. "Stay away from Seth. I don't want you to see him anymore."

"I'm the Voice of God. I can't stay away from the gods."

"I'm a sidhe you're asking not to have sex," he said. "You'd have to be selfish to expect me to commit when you won't do the same."

"There's a difference between selfishness and self-care," Marion said. And right now, what she most needed to do to care for herself was walk away from Konig.

She left him holding vigil alone. One last moment with Nori before the earth took her body.

Marion wished she could have been angrier about it.

It would have been nice if she'd been angry at all, really.

Yet she was only exhausted.

She walked the empty wing of Myrkheimr for the first time as queen. Not steward, not "princess," but *queen*. The wards didn't speak to her at all. The Winter Court had reluctantly responded to Marion when she'd been the sole ruler, but the Autumn Court had no interest at all. Myrkheimr knew that its prince had risen to become king. It cherished Konig in the way that Marion couldn't.

The throne room was emptier than Marion's heart.

"Queen of nothing," she said, stopping to stand in the burned circle where balefire had been.

"But a queen nonetheless," said someone behind her.

She spun, bow leaping into her hands, an arrow instantly in her fingers.

Marion didn't shoot.

There were two people in the throne room who hadn't been there when she entered. Neither of them belonged, but Marion recognized both.

One of them was a curvaceous woman with mounds of chestnut curls that were streaked with gray near the roots. Her breasts were lifted by a tightly cinched corset dress. She cradled a large glass vessel in her arms, which was filled with some kind of glowing potion that tinted her flesh crimson.

Ariane Kavanagh looked much like Marion, in a way—the same hair, the same graceful way they wore their gowns, the same fierce mischief in their eyes.

And she was standing beside a child-sized demon wearing an orange cloak. When that creature pushed her hood back, she revealed the head of a goat, with large eyes marked by oval pupils. "My name is Onoskelis," said the goat-headed demon. "Your names are Marion Garin, Marion Kavanagh, Queen of the Unseelie, and Voice of God. It's finally time for us to talk again."

Made in the USA
Middletown, DE
27 November 2018